# INVISIBLE TO
# INVALUABLE

# INVISIBLE TO INVALUABLE

*Unleashing the power
of midlife women*

## Jane Evans
### and
## Carol Russell

PIATKUS

PIATKUS

First published in Great Britain in 2021 by Piatkus

1 3 5 7 9 10 8 6 4 2

A CIP catalogue record for this book
is available from the British Library.

ISBN: 978-0-34942-859-8

Typeset in Sabon by M Rules
Printed and bound in Great Britain by Clays Ltd, Elcograf S.p.A.

Papers used by Piatkus are from well-managed forests
and other responsible sources.

MIX
Paper from
responsible sources
FSC® C104740

Piatkus
An imprint of
Little, Brown Book Group
Carmelite House
50 Victoria Embankment
London EC4Y 0DZ

An Hachette UK Company
www.hachette.co.uk

www.littlebrown.co.uk

*This book is dedicated to*
*Verna Wilkins, who taught us how to fight with a pen,*
*and Mavis Russell, who armed Carol for the fray.*

# INCLUSIONS

# INTRODUCTION

## *The women of our time*

Have you ever read something so beautiful and thought-provoking you had to stop everything and sit with it for a while?

In the early days of lockdown, when everyone was in a state of shock, two storytellers stopped, sat in the sunshine, marvelled at the birdsong we never usually got to hear and pondered the words of a great African American poet who took our breath away:

> *Normal never was. Our pre-corona existence was not normal. Other than we normalised greed, iniquity, exhaustion, depletion, extraction, disconnection, confusion, rage, hoarding, hate and lack.*
>
> *We should not long to return, my friends. We are being given a chance to stitch a new garment. One that fits all of humanity and nature.*
>
> – Sonya Renne Taylor

The reason why these words held so much power for us at the start of lockdown was because they were the sentiments we'd been trying to express for years. We knew a change was coming but we didn't know the form it would take. We'd discussed the future at length, Jane, the optimist who jumped into the tech startup world with awe and Carol, with her down-to-earth sense of community, questioning where we'd all fit in.

We never imagined it would be a pandemic that would herald the clash between the old and the new. Old systems – new tech, old energy sources – new renewable energy, old ideas – new concepts. Old and new, left and right, Black and white, man and woman, young and old.

No middle anywhere.

Except us. Women aged between 45 and 70 are both young and old; we have a life well lived and have half a life to create. We are past our childbearing years with a quarter of a century of work years ahead. But we don't exist. We're skipped over. The stages of a woman's life are depicted in the media as:

- Little girl
- Troubled teenager
- Sex object
- Career woman
- Mum
- Old woman waiting to die

It's not the media's fault we don't exist, it runs much deeper than that: it's societal. Ageism is first detected in children as young as three. And who can be surprised when they are fed a constant diet of old hags and witches?

It gets even uglier with all the airbrushing, body-shaming and female competition that's inflicted on us from our teens. It's no wonder it all rises to a climax of Botox, fillers, skin lighteners and laser skin removal at the first sign of a wrinkle or age spot.

We're taught to fear the passage of time, not celebrate it.

And we're not even old.

A more realistic image of today's older women would not be as a wicked witch or sweet old granny, it would be as a mum. We're having kids later, with a hell of a lot of us full-on parenting till well into our sixties. And we're doing a hell of a lot more than that too.

This book is a celebration of what midlife women do, who we are, what we are capable of and how much we have to give the world. It's a mishmash of the conversations we have had over the years, with stories and observations of the women who surround us and of those who came before us. Both of us have written with a pile of much-loved and well-thumbed books beside us that tell the stories of the history and culture that shaped us, as well as the myths that defined us. We share the stories of women we admire, ideas and research that excite us and a few tweets that made us laugh along the way.

Both of us are now uninvisible. But we're not writing our stories as a guide to how we became seen and heard. We're all part of the uninvisibility story and we're writing to show that even if we feel like we've hit rock bottom or have disappeared entirely, there *is* a way back for all of us. Our own personal experiences and situations vary wildly. This book is a call for us all to come together by recognising our strengths and talents, to make a difference in our own worlds with our own words.

For those who are delicate about swearing. Sorry. We believe in freedom of expression so you may have to pardon our French at times.

And yes, we are challenging the old systems. This book travels from the start of time to the start of the future. We joke it's a guide to dismantling the patriarchy by the women who made it wobble. The saddest thing about the invisibility of our incredible generation is no one knows our stories and how much we've achieved. We know it's possible to change the world; we've never stopped. We've even got the baddies on the run . . .

*'It's not Me Too. It's not just sexual harassment.*
*It's an anti-patriarchy movement.*
*Time's up on 10,000 years of recorded history.*
*This is coming. This is real.'*

– Steve Bannon

# 1

# INVISIBLE

## *The return of the invisible women*
## *Jane Evans*

In 2018, I saw a magnificent woman on the tube. I'm pretty sure nobody else saw her. She was in her 50s, with bright purple hair, Doc Martens and a pack of Tena Lady pads perched proudly on her lap. I laughed. She had my respect. She knew it. She actually started a movement. You see, she caught me at the peak of my invisibility, at the point I was about to give up.

I had tried for three years to get a job in the ad industry. An industry I had starred in for over thirty years. An industry that claimed to be taking seriously the fact that in 2015 only 3% of the world's creative directors (the people who ultimately decide what we see in commercials) were women. I was the most ridiculously over-qualified candidate: I had created some of Australia's most loved brands and campaigns, had a bank of awards and had run my own agency with clients like Revlon and Maserati. I was back in London where I started my career, with glowing recommendations from global heads of companies. I'd seen headhunters who would say how desperately the industry needed female leadership, only to never hear from them again.

In those three years, I applied for something like 180 jobs and went for a total of 5 interviews. I was met with comments like: '*I'd give you a job but you'd end up the old woman at the back of the creative department doing the shit no one else wants.*' Or, '*We'd give you the job but we think you'd be bored*'. And my personal favourite, '*He was excited by your 50-something female awesomeness. But there was not enough super-current, big-thinking, innovation-centric, high-level conceptual, tech-friendly work.*' Whatever that means.

My industry has changed. It has fallen in love with data and digital natives and fetishises youth. The average age in an ad agency is 33.9 and the thought of a midlife woman in their midst horrifies them. I started my career with the fabulous author and producer Joan Ellis. When she embarked on a new copywriting job in her early 50s, the young male creative team quipped '*Is it bring your granny to work day?*' As Joan recounted the story, we both sort of laughed, then sighed. We were both the first girls in our respective creative departments. We were pioneers when it really was the Wild, Wild West. Naturally, all that sexism and misogyny we'd faced was 'just a joke'. We really did try to smile more.

But we're way too old for drama these days and we're not putting up with ageism. We just roll up our sleeves. '*I had them eating their words within a week,*' Joan said with the complete lack of imposter syndrome that can only come with decades of experience.

Experience that tells us the ad industry hasn't changed; it's just lost the plot.

I've always believed that my job is to tell cool stories that get people to buy stuff – and the fact is women over 45 buy 50% of everything. So, surely clients should be interested in the people who buy half their stuff? So I took out a loan, went to every startup incubator in London and started a new agency, thinking I had the magic formula.

I didn't.

I was enthusiastically introduced to the head of planning at a major brand. I had the coolest influencer on board, with a massive cross-generational audience, who had a huge year coming up. This was the young exec's response to my introduction:

*'Just want to be upfront about this which is our target consumer is 19 and under. If anything, we will be going younger. That's not to say the mature market isn't interesting and important to us but we have to prioritise based on our strategic goals.'*

It seems the under-19 market is more important to marketers than the women who pay for almost everything for the under 19s, what's more, they don't even have time to talk to us.

I knew right then and there I was a goner. I'd tried everything. I couldn't repay the loan and my landlady was about to issue an eviction notice.

Then I saw the punk Tena Lady on the tube, I knew I was the only one who spotted her and I knew I was the only one who noticed what was sitting on her knee and the message she was sending. At that precise moment I knew the universe had dropped the storyteller in the middle of the story.

And what a story. I have travelled from having a cup of tea at the foodbank to high tea at St James's Palace.

Since 2015, I have been to places no female advertising creative ever goes – let alone comes back from, such as the Job Centre and being 'coached' by one of their business mentors; applying for housing benefits (honestly, I have applied for multi-million-dollar mortgages that had less paperwork and stress) and spending a few days in the Maudsley Psychiatric Hospital in South London. Believe it or not, that situation is only about the third stickiest I have found myself in. I am no stranger to waking up in a mental hospital, piecing together how I got there. I rarely talk about my mental illness and I never give it a name. My psychiatrist puts it best: 'In ancient times you'd be sat in the middle of the village and protected till the visions subside.' I do not know why I have visions that sometimes make it impossible to live in modern society, but I do know the trigger – men fucking with my career. After my third visit to the psych ward, it wasn't hard to work out precisely when and how patriarchal sexism had knocked me out this time. The way I survived those mornings of waking up in a psych ward is exactly the way I handled finding myself at the food bank. '*Stop. Take a big deep breath. Look around you. Listen. Now, why are you here?*'

A couple of years into my unemployment, as I sat clutching a couple of much-needed plastic bags in a local church with a very lovely white middle-class Christian woman praying for me, I realised I was the only woman with all my teeth and the only one with the ability to get out. Even though the ham sandwiches, sponge cake and tea were manna from heaven and, as a single menopausal mum of girls going through puberty, a month's worth of tampons, pads and deodorant were a godsend, I swore I was getting out and never coming back. More than that, I was damned well going to make sure I could stop as many other women in my position from needing to be there either.

Because the worst thing about invisibility is you think you're alone. It's easy to believe you're worthless and, in some perverse way, maybe even think you deserve it. That's what goes through the minds of all abused women. And we're a generation abused by the patriarchy because they 'let us in' (well, us white girls, anyway), but made absolutely no concessions to accommodate us. We were allowed on the pitch, but no one told us the rules. We had to make it up as we went along, all while playing on the slanted side with the sun in our eyes. Only the toughest survived and you just have to hear a few of our #MeToo stories to know many of us lived through a nightmare.

Now women over 55 are the biggest group of female suicides in the UK. That's a figure you just don't hear and it's the ultimate cost of invisibility. No one knows or cares when we disappear.

But we don't have to.

It's physically impossible to be invisible anyway and it's a lot like being pregnant – once you're in the same situation, all of a sudden, the world seems to be filled with women just like you. In the early days of the Uninvisibility project I was having a meeting with a young female PhD student who was working on wearable tech for older women (I know, I'm over 50, I'm not even supposed to know what wearable tech is). During a lull in our conversation, the well-dressed attractive woman on the table next to us sighed deeply, took a sip of her cappuccino and said to her obvious life-long best friend; 'Well, the interview went really well, but I know they'll give it to some 30-year-old.' The friend didn't contradict her or give her useless platitudes. We all just sat there in the glaring silence of an unfair truth.

That's a silence that shouldn't be there. I may have been invisible to people who could employ my talents. But I could never be invisible to the people who really know what I'm capable of. There is one place on this earth where I have been shouting my journey of under-employment from the rooftops: Twitter. It didn't take me long to build a following of influential women to start the ball rolling.

The Uninvisibility Project began with a tweet to see if there are actually any women over 50 who are employed full-time to create ads in London agencies. It was retweeted 64 times and greeted with responses like, *'Hen's teeth and unicorn tears easier to find!'* and *'Good luck with that!'*

From that tweet, I got eight names. Now, there may be a few more creative women who are afraid to tell the industry their age, which is sad, because we become even more invisible when we deny our own existence.

Fortunately, four of the eight agreed to tell their stories and were very candid. But there were a lot of stories they could not tell. Three of the four women were under gag orders. In fact, between those four women, there had been no less than eleven legal actions. '*I wasn't fighting for my career, I was fighting for my rights,*' says Janetta Lewin, a woman who learnt her trade at London's Royal College of Art in the 1960s and is still the coolest cat you could hope to meet. But she can't tell you what she experienced, what she did about it, why she did it or how she successfully litigated. Women like Janetta may be visible, but they've been silenced. They fought sexual harassment and assault, bullying, ageism and stolen ideas, but they can't tell us how. They don't want to speak for retribution, they want the gag orders removed so they can tell their stories to ensure the women who follow them don't share the same discrimination and abuse.

The saddest thing about their stories is every woman thought she was alone in her experience. I knew they weren't. And I knew this wasn't just an advertising tale. I reached out and found eleven more women, from comedians and models to the indomitable sex tech pioneer Cindy Gallop and a swimming teacher from Brixton, who told their inspiring and powerful stories.

Forty days (and forty nights) after the initial tweet, I single-handedly launched the Uninvisibility Project. I found 15 women, wrote their stories, photographed them, built a website, created a social media campaign, got a couple of PR pieces and #uninvisibility had over two million views in our first week alone.

The Uninvisibility Project went from strength to strength, our audience grew rapidly and were highly involved. We joked we weren't building an audience but recruiting an army. Almost a year into the campaign, we had started to change the narrative, but no one was prepared to put their money where our mouth was. We had to run a GoFundMe to survive; one of the brilliant women on our site couldn't pay her rent. Another was filing for bankruptcy but couldn't afford the filing fee. And one was being evicted. Me.

THEN. EVERYTHING. CHANGED.

The world stopped and took a breath.

Covid gave everyone an opportunity to look at the world through a new lens. When the first lockdown started, this book was already written and on its final edit. I tore it up. Because ideas that were previously pure hypotheses – like running a home is like running a business – were now being perfectly illustrated by our shared experience. In our pandemic world, life has changed. Business has changed. We have changed.

This coming together has also allowed us to recognise the experiences we do not share. Black Lives Matter made us all listen. Of course, some will always be too stupid or selfish to care. But everyone got the message and it is crystal clear. Even those of us who pride ourselves on our inclusivity quickly changed our course to represent and collaborate with our exhausted Black friends, colleagues and allies.

Meet Carol Russell. One of my best friends in the whole wide world.

I first met Carol in 2014 when we sat next to each other in a writers' room at the National Film and Television School (NFTS). I had just arrived back in the UK and was trying my hand at writing things a little longer than 30 seconds. Carol was already a highly experienced TV writer; she'd enrolled in the Write the Pilot course to force herself to sit down without distractions to damned well get her latest brilliant script down on paper. After hearing the writers pitch their projects we were both attracted to each other's ideas, both were high concept supernatural stories set in the real world. But it was over a cup of tea, we really bonded over a shared recognition of the universe working overtime. I made the classic white girl mistake of asking my new Black acquaintance if she knew another Black friend of mine. But this wasn't just any old friend; this was a woman who had played a massive part in forming my view of the world. I felt blessed to have grown up next door to her. She was my hero. It turned out Carol didn't just know her, she knew her well. This remarkable shared connection became a cornerstone of the new book.

For the last six years Carol and I have had a pact: we only answer the phone to each other if we have a couple of hours to spare. We have stories to share and new worlds to create. We could natter for days about our characters, our plots and our lives. All completely intertwined as the best stories always are.

But nobody wanted to hear them.

I watched Carol work on project after project that fell in a heap because white people kept telling her what her story should be. She watched me fight for my career as young white people told me it was over.

We understood that, even though our lives were different and our experiences poles apart, we both shared the frustration of being midlife women in a world that had no use for us.

So now we're sitting down and turning those six years of phone calls putting the world to rights into words.

*Invisible to Invaluable* has been written with joy, as the world moves beneath our feet. We know the next few years are going to be challenging, and change can mean a cruel roll of the dice for many. But with a whole new world to create, this book is a call for the world to start to see us and a rallying cry for the generation of women who have changed the world before: it's time to step up to the plate and do it again.

But this time it's for real.

# 2

# INAUDIBLE

## *The unheard woman roars*
## *Carol Russell*

One of the most common complaints about me to my parents when I was in primary school was, put bluntly by the teacher who didn't like me, 'Carol talks too much!' Those teachers called me disruptive and told my parents that I wouldn't let the other children do their work. What none of them could ever say though was that I hadn't done my work. The teachers who liked me put it this way, 'Carol's a bit of a chatterbox.'

There was one teacher, Sister Bernadette, who adored me, and I her. She understood me. Sister Bernadette, who I had twice in primary school – once in Year 2, and then again in Year 6 – loved my enthusiasm. She also understood that I wasn't just chatting to the other kids at my desk, I was trying to help them with their work. What she also knew was that I needed more work – more challenging work. But she wouldn't have disagreed with the teachers who said I talked – a lot.

She was also the teacher who persuaded the headteacher to allow me to put on a play in Year 3. It was *The Emperor's New Clothes*. I wrote it. Directed it. Was the titular Emperor. And even organised the costumes – yes, including the 'nude' costume, which consisted of the white vest and navy blue knickers we had to wear for PE. It was a hit and the other kids talked about it for days after. That should have told me I was going to train as an actor/director and become a playwright and a screenwriter.

So, you can imagine what it's been like to discover that I am inaudible.

Looking back, my inaudibility began when I hit puberty. I was a girl and I was Black in Britain, which meant that none of the career avenues open to my white school friends were open to me. Then a wonderful thing happened – work with me now. The beginning of this story doesn't sound too promising, but it does get better.

I was 13 years old and I had come top in the end of year exams for the second year running, which dragged me out of the bottom stream of my year – which I shouldn't have been in – up through the middle and into the top stream. And for this feat, my father had bought me a Parker fountain pen. I loved that pen. Back in the day, it was the pen of pens! The following term, because of my position in my year's rankings, I got to choose which subjects I was going to take, and I was guaranteed to be in the top stream. One of the subjects I chose was chemistry, and as I was in the top stream I was taught by Miss Stephenson. I'll never forget her name.

We were six weeks into the first term, and I'd noticed that Miss Stephenson had exactly the same pen as me as she marked some of my work. Her pen even had her name engraved on it in silver. It made me really proud that we had the same pen. I can't remember how long after I noticed that we had the same pen, but Miss Stephenson and the head-teacher, Sister Mary-Joseph, came into one of my classes and she pointed to the pen I had in my hand saying, 'There it is. That's my pen.' In front of everyone in my class. I tried to explain that it wasn't her pen. It was my pen. That my father had bought it for me as a present. But I didn't get very far. She wasn't listening.

Seems I was inaudible.

Sister Mary-Joseph took the pen out of my hand and handed me a letter to my parents with an appointment to see her at the end of the week.

That evening after school, I prepared an evening meal seasoned by my tears. My parents were going to kill me. As immigrants, the last thing they needed was to take time off work because I'd somehow got myself in trouble. I gave my mother the letter after she'd finished her meal and she went ballistic. My father arrived soon after and he was more measured. He asked why they had to turn up at my school and I explained about the pen and the mistake I knew had been made. I ended my explanation with, 'Miss Stephenson's pen has her name on it: Christine Stephenson.' My father told my mother not to worry, he would go to the school to keep the appointment. So, she didn't have to book time off.

I didn't know what the plan was. All I knew was that I wasn't dead.

A few days later I was called out of class to go to Sister Mary-Joseph's office and when I got there my dad was waiting for me. I wasn't there but a minute before we were called into her office. Miss Stephenson was there, stood on Sister Mary-Joseph's right-hand side. Hands clasped grimly in front of her. Lips pursed.

My father extended his hand. It wasn't taken. He sat before being asked. I sat beside him. As Sister Mary-Joseph laid out the accusations against me, I snuck a glance at Miss Stephenson: she looked furious and smug. When Sister Mary-Joseph was done, my father asked to see the pen. He explained that he had bought one for me that was exactly like this one. 'I have the receipt for it.' Then he took out his wallet, removed a receipt from it. Put it on the table and slid it over to Sister Mary-Joseph. As she was looking at it, he said to Miss Stephenson, 'I understand that your pen has your name, Christine Stephenson, I believe, engraved on it. Is that right?' When she said yes, he turned the pen in his hand, examining the smooth petrol blue surface, and then said, 'Right, so could you explain to me how my daughter removed your name from this pen and managed to re-polish it like new?'

I can never be sure what happened in that room next because I was sent out to wait for my father. When he eventually came out of the office, he had my pen in his hand. He told me to go and get my bag and he took me with him to work. That night I overheard a conversation between my parents and heard my father say, 'You see how it's going, Mavis. We cannot allow them to criminalise our children. If I hadn't had the receipt to show the headmistress, they would have called the police on her.'

A few short months after that I was on a plane with my mother and brother to Jamaica.

Now Jamaica wasn't perfect. To this day, it carries the scars of colonialism on its body and in its people, like many ex-colonies. But after the initial shock of leaving my friends and father behind, I quickly settled into the place where my confidence grew with each and every day – even with the other prejudices that were present due to our colonial history.

For seven brilliant years, I wasn't inaudible.

But after studying at the Jamaica School of Drama in the Cultural Training Centre (now the Edna Manley College of Visual and Performing Arts), I returned to the UK. To a UK which was just about to explode due to so-called 'Race Riots' in 1981. A UK where those who had been inaudible were continuing in the footsteps of those who raised their voices to fight for our rights as women *and* people of African descent.

That I am still inaudible today is a testament to the enduring power of sexism and racism. These days there's a word for that – misogynoir, an ingrained prejudice against women who are Black. Add ageism and classism to that, you've got a full house.

BUT!

And that's a big but . . . I've never been one to just lie down and take it. The women whose shoulders I stand on have never just taken it. Even when we were forced to work in the fields of America and the Caribbean, we looked for ways to resist and found them. It's said that you can't get over a wrong until it's been named, acknowledged and owned, because if you can't say what you're fighting against, you can't change it. I would add that if you see things you can do to make a material difference, give it a go. At the very least, it's action, not suffering in silence.

Which leads me to talking about the actions I'm taking today. Unlike my friend, Jane, I didn't suddenly hit an age and become inaudible. Those of us who have grown up in families of African descent, or ethnically diverse families, have all heard the saying, 'You'll have to work 10 times as hard to get half as far as your white counterparts.' Some of us didn't want to believe our parents when they told us this, but we soon learnt the truth of it as we left school and tried to get into arenas we hadn't traditionally been a part of, like the creative entertainment industries.

After training in Jamaica and returning to the UK, I tried for three years to get an Equity card so that I could audition for work as an actor. The main problem was there weren't many parts for people of African descent at the time. But eventually I got a job in a small company that had a card it could give to a new actor. Hurrah! I thought I was set up. No.

Theatre is a harsh master. While the work came, especially in theatre in education, community theatre and small scale touring companies, the pay was not good. You couldn't feed a gerbil on what actors were paid in theatre. The money was in TV adverts and drama and the joke amongst Black actors was if you were male your best chance of getting a job was as 'The Accused' in the police drama *The Bill*, and if you were a woman, the role was 'Mother of the Accused'. For anything other than that, there were five female actors who tended to get those jobs, and I wasn't one of them.

So, in the mid-to-late 1990s, after working as an actor for 13 years I decided to try my hand as a writer. I figured it couldn't be harder than trying to be an actor. I started telling everyone who would listen that I was a writer and one day, to my utter surprise, I got a call from Paulette Randall, a writer/director I knew who was working for Sir Lenny Henry's company, Crucial Films. There was an offer of a job if I could come up with an idea for a short script as part of a series called *Still Here*, commissioned to celebrate the 50th anniversary of the *Windrush* landing. While we were on the phone, an idea jumped into my head, my episode was called *House of Usher*, about a young woman of African-Caribbean descent who was determined to see the R'n'B singer Usher.

That short, 10-minute script opened doors and windows for me, which included co-writing two seasons of the TV-ratings smash *Comin Atcha*, a vehicle for pop group Cleopatra, signed by Madonna's record label. Next up was being invited onto the writing team behind the BAFTA-nominated adaptation of Jacqueline Wilson's *The Story of Tracy Beaker*.

My agent was so pleased with me, every time she put me up for a writing job, or to meet with production companies about my own series ideas, 7 out of 10 times I'd get a meeting. This is more like it, I thought. But five years in and the whole thing ground to a halt – and not just for me. In the space of a couple of years, the writing jobs dried up for women writers of African and Asian descent. From the early to mid 2000s, some of us managed to get the odd gig on the continuing dramas, also known as soaps, but creating original series or working on the big 9 o'clock shows were no longer in our reach. And this wasn't about merit. We'd been getting the jobs, writing the scripts, getting good reviews. It seemed that Black and Brown folk were no longer in fashion.

But there is more than one way to skin a cat. For years, I banged on doors and thrust my scripts into producers' hands. What they told me time after time was that the commissioners thought there was no audience for work like mine about families, lawyers, midlife women, female friends – or anything that wasn't about the tiny percentage of young people of African and African-Caribbean descent who die at the hands of gangs.

So I decided to try something new.

In 2011, I set up my company, Fresh Voices UK. I raised some money and used my BAFTA membership to pry open some doors. I decided to get a group of actors together to present a 'script in hand' performance at BAFTA for an audience of producers from production companies who make shows, and commissioners, the people who make the decision about what will be shown on TV. And I went further. I also decided to invite an audience of ordinary people to watch this performance. And I put together a panel of a writer, a director and a BBC commissioner to give their feedback on the script. I held a series of these events to demonstrate to the TV industry that there was an audience that wasn't all Black and Brown, but a truly racially mixed audience, who wanted to see work that showed Britishness in all its glory.

It worked.

The industry turned up. The audience came out. The script was a hit. We went from putting on performances to working with Directors UK, the national association for screen directors, putting them together with writers; there was an event at ITV with guest CEO Andy Harries – who'd given me my second commission – and a series of Boot Camps for writers, supported by Skillscreen and the London Film School, to help

writers of African and Asian descent put together that killer
original script needed to get work in the industry. We started a
movement eventually picked up by the rest of the industry. In
2021, as I write, we've come a long way from that half a dozen
writers of African and Asian descent working on continuing
dramas. Our writers now work all over the world.

And now, it's time to do the same thing for midlife women
of African descent.

The stories by midlife women of African descent are
rarely told in film or television, but they are occasionally
told in theatre. And I know TV production companies love
playwrights – what's not to love? We create great characters
and explore big ideas. And I've never met a TV exec who
didn't love a big idea. So in 2019, I created a project, Raised
Voices, to amplify the plays of women of African descent
over 45. I enlisted the help of a friend who helped shape the
project, persuaded two theatres in London to support the
project, before applying to the Royal Society of Literature for
a Literature Matters Award. As Covid-19 hit the UK and we
went into the first lockdown, we heard we'd got the award.
Then we heard the theatres were closing. But we know that
project is just postponed, not cancelled.

We thought we'd have to wait for another day to be heard.
In the meantime, to paraphrase the words of the 1939
British government WWII motivational poster, we'd keep
writing and supporting each other and carry on until the
theatres reopen.

Then. Everything. Changed.

'I CAN'T BREATHE!'

Those three words reverberated around the world.

Those of us who had heard those words before from Eric
Garner, in 2014, were haunted by the similarity. We'd seen
the smartphone footage of a NY police officer holding him
in a choke-hold then. This time we heard them from George

Floyd, another African American man begging for his life, on 25 May 2020, as three policemen knelt on him for eight minutes and forty-six seconds – one of them on his neck. After 8.46, he was dead. His death, like Eric Garner's, was captured on smartphones, the mainly Black people filming the incident pleading with the police to get off his neck and let him breathe.

George Floyd's death sparked outrage in the hearts of people of African descent in America and Europe. We all knew why he had died like that, in the street calling for his mama. The footage flew around the world from smartphone to smartphone and the outrage grew as we heard about Breonna Taylor, who'd been shot in her bed eight times in March. And before we could recover, we heard about Ahmaud Arbery, chased by three men in two flat-bed trucks and shot dead in the street, that on my birthday, 23 February.

Our outrage poured out into the streets, where we were joined by a diverse group of people protesting George's death and the death of all the men and women killed at the hands of the police as we screamed –

BLACK LIVES MATTER!

And our brothers and sisters in the human race around the world joined us, adding their voices, picking up that rallying cry like a baton. Adding their voices to ours so the cry could not be ignored. In the words of the Sam Cooke song my mother would play as we cleaned the house on a Saturday morning – 'It's been a long time coming, but I know a change is gonna come.'

I think the message is finally getting through.

But we have to keep our foot on the gas, because people of African descent have been here before. We've heard the 'outpourings' of support and claims of allyship, and a few short months later it's back to the status quo. And that's because racism and sexism and ageism are systemic and what we've got to be prepared to do is smash the system and build a new one.

And if that is to happen there's going to be much talking and a lot of listening. Women of African descent cannot continue to be inaudible if all women are to rise.

# 3

# INQUISITION

## *Time to question everything*

July 2020

> CAROL
>
> What's a good place to start making
> things better for midlife women?

> JANE
>
> Well when did it start getting
> bad for us?

> CAROL
>
> How far do you want to go back?

'In the beginning, God made the heavens and the earth.' Did he? There isn't a scientist, anthropologist, or archaeologist on this planet who believes the world was built in seven days back in 3761 BC. But the story persists to this day, even though it wasn't written down until the reign of King David somewhere around 1000 BC when it was considered a new idea.

The majority of creation stories prior to this told of a world ruled by the feminine, and yet somehow these oral stories are now branded as nothing more than myths and fantasy. There are figurines of goddesses that date back 25,000 years but most modern societies believe men have always run the world without question.

It was questioned!

### The Queen of Sheba

Mystery surrounds the 'Queen of the South' mentioned in the Bible, Talmud and Koran. She may be Bilqis, the great queen of the land we now call Yemen. However, recent DNA testing appears to show she is more likely to be Makeda, the African Queen of Ethiopia. Other theories claim she is pure allegory; 'sheba' is the word for 'seven' in Hebrew and Freemasons believe she is a symbol of the Queen of Heaven. Whether fable or fact, one thing's for sure, when a powerful African ruler heard that a prosperous king named Solomon from a tiny desert land believed in a male god and was being touted as the wisest man on earth, she had questions.

She couldn't believe a man could hold that much power.

Sheba ruled a vast land, worshipped the sun and she was an all-powerful virgin queen – which had a whole different meaning 3,000 years ago – she could have all the sex and all the children she wanted, but she couldn't take a husband. No man could be her equal.

There are fantastical stories of Makeda sending 6,000 young men and women, each born on the same hour of the same day, to hand-deliver her RSVP to Solomon's arrogant summons to learn his wisdom. But the Old Testament sets out her power in no uncertain terms. When Solomon answered her questions, she gifted him with spices, precious jewels and a hundred and twenty talents of gold. At that time, a talent was based on the weight of a person. In today's terms Sheba's gift would be worth somewhere around $120 million.

*'She came to Solomon and talked with him about all that she had on her mind. Solomon answered all her questions; nothing was too hard for the king to explain to her.'*

1 Kings 10

The Bible never explains Sheba's questions. In the Middle Ages, writers pondered what she would have asked of Solomon, they created stories of riddles and trifles like telling an identically dressed boy and girl apart or discerning a real flower from an identical fake.

Other stories talk of Sheba arriving at Solomon's court to find a specially constructed glass floor flooded to a mirror-like sheen with water. (If this is true it's probably the world's first case of upskirting.) The ruse was a way to look at her legs, which were reportedly hairy and hooved like a goat. Of course a powerful Black queen would have been depicted as a she-devil back then.

A far more rational and historically correct scenario is Sheba questioned an equal on a whole new belief system – something new was coming and she had to reconcile it with everything she knew so far. And if Solomon was the wisest man on earth, he'd certainly have the sense to listen to a strong Black queen. Women's oral stories tell of Sheba discussing life, love and the universe with Solomon before taking him to make a sacrifice at the temple of Isis who is nature, the parent of things, and the queen of all elements.

Some say it was nothing more than discussions between two heads of state. Others believe it was the greatest love story of all time.

One thing is known. Makeda arrived home and gave birth to a son. Emperor Menelik started an empire that would crumble due to famine during the reign of Emperor Haile Selassie some 225 generations later. A dynasty whose very name gives credence to the reports that Menelik visited his father. The Solomite dynasty ended in 1974.

One myth is the young African king came to steal the Ark of the Covenant, the fabled golden chest that houses the two stone tablets of the Ten Commandments. Ethiopians believe it was given as a gift and claim to guard it to this day. Others say Menelik was summoned with a group of wise men to learn Solomon's secrets and spread them across the globe.

Did those secrets contain what Solomon learned from a wise woman steeped in the ways of nature who also wielded the power of story? Sheba almost certainly changed the King of the

Hebrews and challenged their 'jealous' new God. Solomon was practically excommunicated for lighting incense and sacrificing to 'gods' of his enemies.

*'And the Lord was angry with Solomon, because his heart was turned from the Lord God of Israel.'*

1 Kings 11:9

The Bible blamed his 'strange wives' for turning away his heart. They say he had hundreds of wives and concubines, but did his heart truly belong to just one?

We don't know if the Ark of the Covenant was stolen or gifted or if it were real at all. Some say it is nothing more than the whispered secrets of God only to be revealed through the fabric of time. Another name for this sacred object is the Ark of the Testimony. Did Solomon pass on this sacred testimony to his son the Solomite king with the added instruction to listen to wise women as well? That maybe there are two sides to every story? Maybe it didn't matter whether the boy was a girl or which flower was fake. Maybe we were always supposed to be equals?

For many women of our generation reading all this, you may think we've started out a bit 'woo woo', but ask yourself this, when you were a girl and you asked for something beautiful or extravagant or something your parents couldn't afford, did they say;

*'Who do you think you are? The Queen of Sheba?'*

And let's be honest, if they did, whose immediate thought was 'Um yes, of course!'?

Whether Bilqis or Makeda or both, the Queen of Sheba shared the DNA of an African woman who lived 200,000 years ago. We too share her DNA and it's time for us to draw upon the regal power in each of us. We may have grown up to have very little or possess fortunes beyond our wildest dreams, but let's not underestimate how precious the gifts are that we bring to the world. As in Solomon's time, the world is changing: he brought a God of intellect to a world that worshipped Mother Earth; we face a world where technology changes how we think and behave. Something new has arrived and we have to reconcile it with everything we know so far. We have to ask questions. We have to listen. We have to stand up for what we believe.

We've seen more than most. It's time to speak up and share our wisdom when we all need to see the world with fresh eyes and open hearts.

# 4

# INTERCONNECTED

## *The past is the way to the future*

March 2019

> JANE
>
> Look, I know a whole heap of colonial
> bullshit is coming out of my mouth
> right now. But if I'm going to be inter-
> viewed about all midlife women I've
> got to get it all out, work out where
> it comes from, what it means and what
> the fuck to do with it.

(Carol rolls her eyes, sucks her teeth and mumbles
something in patois under her breath.)

> CAROL
>
> Come on then.

If all women are to come together to fight the effects ageism
wrapped in misogyny has on all of us, it's important that we
begin by understanding how we connect and how our histories connect.

*'A people without the knowledge of their past history,*
*origin and culture is like a tree without roots'*

Marcus Garvey

Some of what you read here may cause you to feel a little uncomfortable, but stay with us. We're not tackling comfortable subjects. We want to take you with us because the patriarchy has done a number on us all, and one way this has happened is the erasure of women from history.

Most people in Britain have absolutely no knowledge of our history. Most of us don't even know how these four nations – England, Scotland, Wales and Northern Ireland came to be the United Kingdom. How many of us know that the United Kingdom of Great Britain was the political union of the Kingdom of England (which included Wales) and the Kingdom of Scotland which took place on 1 May 1707? How many of us know that Queen Anne, a *woman*, was the first monarch of the new Great Britain? She was an ardent supporter of the Union and in her first speech in the English Parliament, declared it was 'very necessary' to conclude the Union as soon as possible. Pretty remarkable for a woman who went through 17 pregnancies.

Relatively few of us understand how the British Empire created multicultural Britain. We don't all understand that the fact of being a member of the British Empire meant that you were a British subject, no matter the colour of your skin. We don't know that fact gave every member of the Empire the right of abode right here in Britain.

It all began in the fifteenth and sixteenth century, during the so-called Age of Discovery, when the European branch of the patriarchy in the form of Portugal and Spain, travelled the globe and using violence and coercion, took over the lands and peoples they came across, setting up 'empires' as they went. Envious of the great wealth these empires were generating, other European countries, including England, France and the Netherlands also started using violence to acquire foreign lands and set up networks of their own, trading the riches, including people, found in these places. After a series of wars between these major European powers Britain was left the dominant colonial power.

Some of us are only just beginning to learn about the things that happened as a result of that notion of 'Empire' and its impact on the people whose lands were invaded, resources stolen, treasures appropriated. In the case of Africa, her people stolen and enslaved. The fact of 'Empire' created a connection between Britain and the 80 or so countries forged by brutality and a resistance that cannot be broken. We are interconnected. Our histories are interconnected. Our fortunes are also interconnected, but we don't always recognise any of this, because the way we're taught history doesn't allow us to make those connections.

So as we educate ourselves and engage in our joint histories as women, we'll hear and talk a lot about the patriarchy, which leads us to ask, how did that start in the first place?

According to 'The Origins of Sexism', an article by Anil Ananthaswamy and Kate Douglas, human societies weren't always male dominated. They argue that patriarchal systems grew out of patrilocal residence systems, which basically means women most often went to live with their husbands and families and that was the beginning of patriarchy. In these localised systems, the men in the family tended to band together and support each other at the expense of the women from outside the family, leaving them vulnerable.

For most of human history, we've been hunter-gatherers and, if modern hunter-gatherer societies reflect anything of prehistoric societies, it seems the women there had a choice of whether to stay with the family they were born into, leave to go to their husband's family or go somewhere else altogether. American anthropologist Sarah Hrdy says women in those patrilocal residence systems would have had the choice of support from the group they grew up with, or the choice to move away.

One school of thought says the change came about 12,000 years ago when we became farmers and settled in one place. The theory goes, as humans stayed put and had fields and crops to defend, the power shifted to men because they were physically stronger and could defend the 'homestead' from thieves. This theory is supported by a study published in 2004. Researchers at Sapienza University of Rome studied the DNA from the female and male lines from 40 populations from sub-Saharan Africa. What they found suggested that women in hunter-gatherer populations were more likely to stay with their mothers after marriage than women from food-producing populations. It was the opposite for men from agricultural societies, suggesting that the growth of patriarchal societies is connected to settling down in one place and growing the food you need. Maybe us women should have kept it moving.

So that's one theory about the beginning of patriarchal systems, but how many of us know that the enslavement of African women affected the development of the sexist systems of the white patriarchy? And then pitted us against each other so we wouldn't come together to defeat them?

In Christian European medieval societies, white women were equated to the biblical Eve, who of course was held responsible for the expulsion of man from the Garden of Eden. The story of Eve underlined men's belief that women were inferior to them, morally weaker and more likely to tempt them into sin. A woman's place in the world was also dictated by the writings of apostles, such as Paul, who emphasised male authority over women, instructed us to be silent and forbade us from teaching – because of course, if women disagreed with men, that would somehow be tempting them into sin. Again ... Which just goes to show, the men who put these systems into action already recognised our power and were terrified of it.

However, the status of and opportunities open to white women began to expand during and after the Black Death pandemic of 1347–52, which claimed about half of the population of England alone. So many men were killed during that time that women were allowed to take ownership and operation of their husband's businesses. As widows, white women's rights continued to expand. Their independence grew and their financial safety was secured by the businesses or land their husbands left behind. At this time, a daughter could also inherit from her father, though of course there was great pressure on her to marry or take the veil. However, by the late Middle Ages (c. 1300–1500), the growing number of women choosing not to re-marry threatened the status quo of male inheritance practices and eventually laws were passed putting land and property firmly back into the hands of men – even if he was a fourteenth cousin 50 times removed. And the very end of the late Middle Ages coincided with when Europeans first began enslaving and trading African peoples.

As Europeans began to settle in the Americas, institutionalised sexism and racial imperialism formed the basis of the social and political structure in the so-called New World. Initially, relatively few African women were trafficked to the Americas by Europeans. This, and the slaughter of many Native Americans, led to, from the coloniser's point of view, a shortage of workers which led some white male colonisers to encourage, persuade and coerce white women to have sexual relationships with enslaved African men as a way of producing more workers.

However, there were other white men who did not like this idea, and in 1664, in the mid-Atlantic state of Maryland, the first anti-amalgamation law was passed aimed at putting an end to these sexual relationships. They first started by making any white woman who married, or had children by an enslaved African man, enslaved to her husband's master along with her children. Although, the white woman would be freed if her husband died before her. The law was later repealed, and a new law put in its place, which made the woman and her children free.

Realising that the enslavement of African women meant they could be bred, and their children would be free labour, more women were stolen and trafficked to the Americas. Another reason also drove the enslavement of African women and became crucial to plantation owners' plans to make their fortunes – the discovery that in West African societies women were not only under the sexist patriarchal thumb, they were also expected to do all the hard work in their communities. Not only did they have to help the men cut and clear the fields for crops, they also had to do all the planting of the rice, cassava and other ground produce. As well as cutting and carrying wood, carrying water from rivers, cooking and looking after the children and the elders of their communities. For a plantation owner, African women's industriousness made her ideal for working in his fields. So, as far as the plantocracy was concerned, the African woman was the perfect slave. In many ways, she was the perfect woman.

So thanks brothers, fathers and sons, your version of the patriarchy played its part in what happened to African women in slavery too.

Surprised?

Don't be.

I haven't gone into the brutality African women endured at the hands of white men under the chattel slavery system because I don't want to trigger myself, or readers of African descent. But when explored, that brutality exposed the depths

of the misogynistic attitudes of hatred of all women and wom-
en's bodies that prevailed in the New World at that time. A
hatred born of a deep fear and enshrined in fundamentalist
Christian beliefs where women were portrayed as the evil
sexual temptress, the bringer of sin into the world. Sexual
lust originated with her and men were just the victims of her
wanton power. The belief that women were inherently sinful
creatures who were to be considered the architects of men's
moral downfall would make you laugh, if the results hadn't
been so damn dangerous to us all.

To fight this, men instigated laws to govern the sexual
behaviour of white women to make sure we would not be
tempted to stray from the path they made for us to follow. The
punishments meted out to those who overstepped the boundaries men deemed as the women's place were severe. The results
of the Salem Witchcraft trials were an extreme manifestation
of patriarchal society's persecution of women. A message to
all women that unless we stayed in our lane in the passive,
subordinate role assigned to us, we would be punished, even
put to death.

Fundamental Christian colonisers sought to suppress female
sexuality because of their deep fear of sexual feelings. This
intense fear bred feelings of hatred and suspicion of women
because the word from their religious teachers was that sex
was sinful and the route to eternal damnation. As women
were the source of those emotions the fear of women bred in
them misogynistic feelings. In *Troublesome Helpmate*, author
Katharine M. Rogers offers an explanation for the emergence
of misogynistic feelings:

> Of the cultural causes of misogyny, rejection of, or guilt
> about sex is the most obvious. It leads naturally to degra-
> dation of women as the sexual object and projection onto
> her of the lust and desire to seduce which a man must

repress in himself ... Misogyny can also develop as the
result of the idealisation with which men have glorified
women as mistresses, wives, and mothers. This has led to
a natural rejection, a desire to tear down what has been
raised unduly high.

The latter part possibly explains what happened when white
men became more prosperous in the colonies and in the rest of
the British Empire. With the shift away from fundamentalist
Christian doctrines in the nineteenth century, men's perception of women changed from all white women being potential
whores tempting men to sin to them being 'the nobler half of
humanity', whose presence elevated the level of men's thoughts
and feelings, inspiring higher moral impulses. Well ... thank
goodness for that.

The new image of white womanhood was diametrically
opposed to that of Eve. She was depicted as goddess rather
than sinner. She was virtuous, pure, innocent, not sexual and
worldly. White male idealisation of white women as innocent
and virtuous removed the stigma Christianity had put on
them. If, and it's an important 'if', white women expressed
sexual feelings they would be seen as degraded immoral creatures. Remove those sexual feelings and they become worthy
of love, consideration and respect. The price white women had
to pay was giving up natural sexual impulses. Most, under-
standably, eagerly absorbed the sexist ideology white men had
imposed on them that claimed virtuous women had no sexual
impulses, because it was better than the Christian model
used to control them which had made all women evil sexual
temptresses responsible for men's moral downfall. Damn, in
Victorian times, they had to cover the legs of tables so as not to
arouse the male sexual beast and cause him to lose his morals.

Patriarchal systems operate a divide-and-rule strategy setting people against one another, especially women, to prevent

alliances that could defeat them. We've been through a lot together and white women were forced to observe the anti-woman male aggression, sexual exploitation and brutality enacted towards enslaved women. The pain that created between us is one of the things we're working our way through now, and why it is important that we understand how we've been pitted against each other.

The fates of African and white women were interconnected. And they still are. As we are interconnected with all women of colour, all classes in society and all sexual orientations.

Among midlife women of African descent and a large number of our daughters in the West there is a saying, which goes, 'All the men are white, all the women are white and all the Blacks are men'. It came about because historically the politics of female suffrage was white. The patriarchy white women were fighting against was that perpetrated by white men. And women of African descent were marginalised in discussions around race as sexism meant almost all discussions were led by Black men, leaving the needs of African women unserved. This led to Black women feeling and being erased from the conversations about both race and gender.

However, we can fight this division, and we can win. But in order to do this we have to acknowledge, understand, examine and reject the racist and sexist brainwashing that has seen women, not only of African descent, but all women of colour, excluded from the term 'women' in the feminist movement. This historical use of the word 'women' by the feminist movement has seen many women of African descent turn their backs on what they see as the 'white feminist movement'. And even those women of colour who proudly shout their feminist credentials from the mountaintops feel erased by the use of the word 'women' when what the speaker is talking about is something that affects 'white women'.

Amy Parish, from University of Southern California, studies

the bonobo societies which are patrilocal but female dominated. In her article, 'The origins of sexism', she talks of bonobo societies where females have the upper hand because they co-operate and form alliances. She says, 'In dismantling patriarchal systems, solidarity is key', adding 'The goal is to behave with unrelated females as if they are your sisters.'

That last statement may seem too simplistic, because there is an implication that as your 'sister' other women look like you, come from the same social class as you and have the same life experiences as you do. And, of course, we don't. But we can work together to dismantle the patriarchal systems as they operate in all our cultures. As African American feminist bell hooks states in her 1981 book, *Ain't I a Woman: Black Women and Feminism*:

> If women want a feminist revolution – ours is a world that is crying out for a feminist revolution – then we must assume responsibility for drawing women together in political solidarity. That means we must assume responsibility for eliminating all the forces that divide women. Racism is one such force. Women, all women, are accountable for racism continuing to divide us. Our willingness to assume responsibility for the elimination of racism need not be engendered by feelings of guilt, moral responsibility, victimization or rage. It can spring from a heartfelt desire for sisterhood, and the personal, intellectual realization that racism among women undermines the potential radicalism of feminism. It can spring from our knowledge that racism is an obstacle in our path that must be removed. More obstacles are created if we simply engage in endless debate as to who put it there.

One way we can begin to heal the divide between us is to look at one of the things the patriarchy in order to justify the enslavement of African had through slavery.

It is time we consign the idea that all the men are white, all the women are white and all the Blacks are men to the trash, and put our heads together to build a new world where we really see each other and our age doesn't consign us to the trash.

# 5

# INHERITANCE

## *We are all the women who have come before us*

September 2019

INT. BAFTA CINEMA LONDON - EVENING

The titles roll on Brad Pitt's latest movie *Ad Astra*.

> CAROL
> Hmmm, 90 minutes of Brad Pitt in
> extreme close-up. I've had worse
> experiences.

> JANE
> Yep. But aren't you bored of films
> about men with daddy issues?

The audience applauds. The lights come up and a
COMPÈRE takes the stage.

> COMPÈRE
> And here to talk about his latest mas-
> terpiece, director James Grey.

A tall, white, midlife man in jeans and sneakers
walks on stage, takes the applause and sits next to
the Compère.

COMPÈRE

> Welcome, James, I want to kick this off
> with the big question, what was your
> inspiration for the movie?

JAMES

> I was exploring Homer's *Odyssey* from
> the son's perspective.

Carol and Jane sigh in unison.

Have you noticed how Hollywood films all feel the same? It's
because most modern films are largely based on a seven-page
memo attributed to Jeffrey Katzenberg, the ex-Head of Disney.
The reality behind 'A Practical guide to the hero with a thousand faces' is that it was first written as an undergraduate essay
by Christopher Vogler, who discovered that George Lucas had
been influenced by the work of Joseph Campbell when writing
the Star Wars trilogy. Campbell is regarded as the master of
storytelling, he studied the structure of myths and folklore
from all lands, all time and all genders and asserts all mythic
narratives are variations of a single great story which he called
the monomyth. His seminal work, *The Hero with a Thousand
Faces*, explores how this structure works in every great story
from the Great Goddess to *The Great Gatsby*.

Vogler simply applied what fitted to *Star Wars*, which was
every young man's obsession in the 1970s. After college, he
became a story consultant at the Disney company and decided
to dust off his essay and distribute it to the top brass.

And somehow lore became the law of screenwriting. Which

of course it is, but a seven-page memo given to writing rooms filled with people who had all been exposed to exactly the same stories gave us a gazillion re-hashes of classics like Homer's *Odyssey*.

What of the heroine's journey? It started a lot further back than when Greek men first jumped on ships.

In the beginning, women were treated as goddesses on earth possessing magical powers. We bled without dying and miraculously created humans from inside ourselves. Then men did the math and discovered it was their seed that made humans. They rewrote all the stories:

Eve bit the apple. And the pantheon of European goddesses were hunted down. The violent gods of war took over. Powerful women who opposed them were painted as fierce figures of revenge and anger. Like dear, sweet Nemesis, the ancient Greek goddess of justice, who distributed fortune, both good and bad, in proportion to what was deserved. She didn't deserve to be chased across the sky and violently raped by the newly empowered Zeus.

They say history is written by the victors. What they don't say is the past is also passed on through the words of the losers. Those spoken words turn into myths, allegory and archetypes. Archetypes are important; they give us something to aspire to and their stories help unravel the complexity of human existence. The truth of the goddesses may have been manipulated, but their spirit lives on to this very day.

It is only in the time of Homer that Nemesis is depicted as a monstrous all-avenging goddess. Who can blame her? Zeus was the Harvey Weinstein of Ancient Greece: it seems any aspiring goddess was in his perverted sights. Earlier stories show Nemesis as one of two great goddesses. Themis, the daughter of Gaea, Mother Earth, was her partner in creating society. Themis was described as the steadfast one, an unshakeable power, the creator of society and the earth mother

personified. No Olympic event could happen without her blessing and the first-ever temple was built to worship her. One of
Themis's daughters was revolutionary too. She is described
as 'her own maiden self, a stern uncompromising virgin'. Her
name? Dike.

So much of the way the Western world views us, and to some
extent, how we see ourselves, is based on white and Brown
men's stories of vanquishing female power. In her 1981 book,
*Goddesses and Heroines*, Patricia Monaghan tells the stories of
over 1,500 goddesses from around the world, starting from A,
a Chaldean moon goddess, to Zywie, the great Polish goddess
of the living. Of those 1,500 goddesses, 28 were raped – 20
of them Greek and 6 of them were victims of Zeus (including
his own mum).

So it really isn't that radical to say that modern patriarchal
society is built on rape culture when its original 'heroes' would
be joining Harvey in prison if they were around today. On top
of Zeus's six rapes, Apollo had three to his name. The rest fell
prey to Poseidon and his son, Orion and various wind gods.
Except Persephone, the goddess of spring. She was raped by
the god of the underworld and her story bears a striking resemblance to the African goddess Ishtar.

But Ishtar didn't face being raped to bring the vegetation
back to life; she went down to hell for a booty call! Her story
has been kept alive, not by oral storytelling, but through the
ancient art of exotic dance. The 'Dance of the Seven Veils' is
a visual representation of Ishtar's love for the god of plants,
Tammuz. Every winter, he would die and she would go to
hell to bring him back. With every step down, she would strip
away her clothing and every ounce of her being. Her Dream.
Her Reason. Her Passion. Her Bliss. Her Courage. Her
Compassion. Her Knowledge. Once Ishtar was stripped of her
power, Tammuz gave her his. And boy, was it powerful. When
'Salome' or 'that girl' (as described in the New Testament)

performed the dance for her father, King Herod II, he was so enamoured he granted her any desire. She asked for the head of John the Baptist on a silver platter. For that she has been painted (again, mostly in the Middle Ages) as the personification of the lascivious woman, a temptress who lures men away from salvation. A more likely scenario is Salome, which ironically means peace in Hebrew, asked her mum what she should ask for. A queen of the time would certainly know the power of the great goddess Ishtar and wouldn't be too happy with another new male 'messiah' and his disciples. They say never make an enemy of a patient woman. Or a powerful goddess. She will never disappear.

Let's be honest, the modern world didn't deserve to be built to satisfy men's egos and sexual desires. Yet here we are, a couple of million years into human life on earth with only the last twelve thousand or so ruled by the patriarchy – a system built on little more than myths.

Myths that, even when disproved, persisted.

The witchcraft hunts of northern Europe and North America raged from 1450 until 1750, with up to 50,000 women murdered. Originally, men and women who continued to worship their ancient goddesses were the main targets. But when Joan of Arc was burnt at the stake in 1431, she was on a mission from God.

Most witches were good women. Witchcraft was a normal part of everyday life in many communities and the women who practised wicca would today be called naturopaths, herbalists, nurses, doulas and therapists. (And in Joan's case – a saint!)

In 1727, the last woman legally executed for witchcraft in Britain was a Scottish woman called Janet Horne. Her two crimes were having a daughter with deformed hands and feet (apparently she had flown with the devil who'd shod her, or some such rubbish) and showing signs of senility. Janet was stripped, smeared with tar, paraded through the town on a barrel and burnt alive. Her daughter, despite her 'unholy deformity', managed to run away. It wouldn't be until her great-great-great-great-great-great-granddaughters' time that Janet would see some justice. The Witchcraft Act was finally repealed in 1951.

These women may have been forgotten by their descendants, but recent research shows they may have carried the memory of her horrendous experience. Research into epigenetics, relating non-genetic influences on gene expression, shows that trauma attaches or removes chemical tags to our DNA. Tags that can affect our psyche or manifest as physical symptoms and diseases for the next seven generations. Native Americans have always known this; they refer to 'soul wounds', the mental scars of warriors who experienced the full horror of battle which are felt by the tribe for the next seven generations.

This also explains why the colonialised have such a visceral reaction to statues of men who oppressed their forebears. Many people can't understand why we can't all see Churchill as a hero or honour the good works of slave masters and traders. But to those who carry the chemical tags from the trauma of their parents, grandparents and great-grandparents, the pain is fresh and deep.

But it's not just the pain of history we carry. We also bear the legacy of a whole lot of ignorance. Midlife women are only the fourth generation of women who have been taught to read. British girls were only given the legal right to an education in 1880.

*'For most of history, anonymous was a woman.'*

– Virginia Woolf

The patriarchal religions guarded their stories from women. The Torah has been scribed word for word since the time of King David, yet it was forbidden for a single word to be written by a female hand and in many sects still is. In the eighth century, women were writing texts in Latin, many scribes were abbesses and nuns although the credit for their labours was given to their male bosses. Before the twentieth century there were only a handful of women known for writing, mostly women of high birth who could afford an education, many of whom took a male nom de plume to disguise their gender. *Middlemarch* is described as one of Britain's greatest novels and George Eliot one of our most famous authors, but few know her by her real name, Mary Ann Evans. The predominance of male authors and their perceived value persists to this very day; Joanne Rowling was urged by her publisher to use her initials, JK, because boys were unlikely to read Harry Potter if it were written by a woman. Even when she was powerful enough to ignore any instruction, she chose to publish her crime novels under the pen name Robert Galbraith (which seems rather hypocritical when she appears so averse to people identifying as the gender of their choice).

There can be no doubt that the literary canon has been dominated by men for the last 3,000 years. That's a lot of narrative to control and a lot of male gaze to counterbalance. A gaze that appears to go no further than the way we look. A 2019 study by the University of Copenhagen used artificial intelligence to analyse the adjectives used to describe women in 3.5 million books. Here are the top 11:

- Beautiful
- Lovely
- Chaste
- Gorgeous
- Fertile
- Beauteous
- Sexy
- Classy
- Exquisite
- Vivacious
- Vibrant

Now compare how men are described:

- Just
- Sound
- Righteous
- Rational
- Peaceable
- Prodigious

- Brave
- Paramount
- Reliable
- Sinless
- Honourable

If we're going to even out this playing field, we need to be judged for more than youth and beauty. We need to rewrite our story with us as the protagonists. It's time for our ancient wisdom to shine. We may have only had the ability to write en masse for a fraction of history, but our stories have been passed down orally from mother to daughter since the start of time.

Indigenous Australians lived patriarchy-free for almost 80,000 years. They revere the wisdom of older women above all else. When you meet a spiritual First Nation elder in Australia, they will talk to two spirits who sit on your shoulder. So, after a polite greeting, they ignore you and get the lowdown straight from your grandmothers. Many of our generation were lucky to get the lowdown from these incredible women in real life. Our grannies and great-grannies lived through both wars or Partition or Independence. They survived the Spanish flu and the Great Depression.

Many of our mothers lived through air raids, rationing and keeping calm and carrying on.

It's probably why a lot of our generation have kept calm and carried on during Covid.

Because we know in our bones (or DNA) how gentle this radical societal change really is compared to the experience of the women on whose shoulders we stand. When we sent our children to the frontline, we smiled that all they were armed with was a price gun and all they had to 'man' were the tills. Those of us with British mothers and grandmothers alive during the Second World War didn't miss the irony of us conscripting our kids and grandkids to sit on the sofa to blow up imaginary enemies on brightly lit screens. We grew up with stories of blackouts, and sons, brothers, fathers and uncles never coming home. We are daughters of women who grew up never tasting a banana – unless they grew up in Africa, the Caribbean or somewhere tropical. Some of us were alive when rationing ended and most of us were forced to do home economics – banana bread was not a revelation to us. Many of us stored old sheets ready to cut up in case there really was a global shortage of toilet paper because we were brought up with 'waste not want not', 'make do and mend'.

When the world seems so uncertain and many can't see a way forward, those of us in the middle are the perfect bridge between the powerful women of our past and the hopes and dreams of all our daughters and sons.

# 6

# INCOMPARABLE

## *There have never been women like us before*

January 2019

> CAROL
>
> Did you get that job?

> JANE
>
> Yep, right up my alley. They wanted a view of what cities will look like in the future.

> CAROL
>
> What did you write?

> JANE
>
> I wrote about a woman who's one of the last old women. The youth serums that actually work were invented after she got her wrinkles. She's in a driverless taxi explaining to a young girl, who's never seen anyone like her before, why

she's going to Brands Hatch to take a
vintage Maserati out for a spin.

                    CAROL
You think everything will be
driverless?

                    JANE
No doubt, they're saying all truck-
ing will be driverless within ten
years or so.

                    CAROL
What will happen to all the
truck drivers?

                    JANE
And factory workers and pharmacists,
and solicitors and copywriters. AI's
going to do so many of our jobs.

                    CAROL
People need to work, what on earth
are they going to do with us all
when they don't need us to make
their money?

                    JANE
Have you read *Sapiens*?

                    CAROL
Not yet.

                    JANE
It says that something always comes
along every now and again that wipes
out a huge swathe of the population
that forces us to change.

CAROL

Probably be a war then.

JANE

Or a revolution. I'm hoping for the
revolution.

CAROL

Did they like the story?

JANE

Not really. Young people don't like
stories about old women. Not even
really cool ones from the future.

These are unprecedented times. Really? The world has seen
pandemics before. And civil rights protests. And racism. And
populism. And there is certainly nothing new about incom-
petent politicians trying to control us all. But our generation
is something the world has never been seen before – women
born between 1950 and 1975 were pioneers in all areas of
work and society. Yet we have become almost completely
invisible except to our families and friends.

We're not imagining it either, we all have stories of being
ignored in shops or have friends who won't stand anywhere
near the yellow line for fear of being bumped onto the tracks
by a younger person (or anyone who identifies as male). Our
invisibility cloak is real.

The media makes it worse: they have absolutely no idea
who we are. It seems every article or story about midlife
women includes a picture of Helen Mirren. She's beautiful
and inspirational and we love her to bits – but she's *75*. In
reality, midlife women are Gwen Stefani and Missy Elliott,
Jennifer Saunders and Thandiwe Newton. Scary, Baby,
Sporty, Ginger and Posh. That's an awful lot of girl power

going to waste. Or are midlife women about to creep up on everyone ...

There are stories that when the first ships sailed the seas of 'Terra Australis', the native landowners couldn't see ships because they couldn't believe such large vessels could float – when they saw white sails on the horizon it was presumed all they saw were clouds. The 2004 film *What the Bleep Do We Know!?* theorised that humans physically can't see what they believe to be impossible. But there is a simpler explanation: when the Great Southern Land was discovered in 1606 it is quite conceivable the original Australians would have seen ships sail by before. They only armed themselves when the white men landed and posed a threat. Either way, our fleet is on the horizon ...

In the world's defence, it really is no surprise that no one sees us. We're the first generation of women who have lived this long. In 1950, the world average life expectancy was 48. And for white English women, it was 72. Now, the average lifespan for British women is 83.6, many of us are likely to live till 90, and if we're healthy and active, it's not above the realms of possibility we could see 120 years on this planet. We are the first generation to hit long life en masse. We're everything the women from the dawn of time have dreamt we could be. Over 45. Childbirth has taken a massive toll on women, and still does. In the United States, it's the sixth biggest killer of women aged between 20 and 34. About 15 women die in pregnancy or childbirth per 100,000 live births. A century ago it was more than 600 women per 100,000 births. And in the 1600s and 1700s, the death rate was twice that. In the days before birth control, sex was a potential death sentence for women. It's amazing the human race has survived at all.

So here we are now with an unexpected gift – the time, freedom and medical advancements that allow us to achieve more than the women who came before us.

And boy, has the world has given us something to do. At times of change we need women who have seen it all before. And we've not only seen revolutionary change in our lifetimes. We created it.

Most people don't realise how recent our radical evolution is or how long it's taken. White middle-class women were the first to see a change just over 100 years ago in 1919, when Britain passed the Sex Disqualification (Removal) Act. This act allowed women to enter the professions of law, become veterinarians and enter the civil service. The Women's Engineering Society was formed in the same year, and Nancy Astor became the first female MP. Yet women were still expected to give up their jobs when they got married. It was only when the 1975 Sex Discrimination Act made it illegal to discriminate against women in employment, education and training that we were legally entitled to join the workforce on an equal basis. Before this a married woman couldn't even open a bank account in her own name or apply for a credit card or loan.

For those who believe legislation was the only barrier to our brilliance or perceive our lived experience as ancient history, we defy you to not sing along with the mixtape of our generation's journey.

British women got the pill in the UK in 1961 as Elvis asked, 'Are You Lonesome Tonight?'. But single women had to wait till ABBA met their 'Waterloo', in 1974, for all of us to take control of our ovaries. It changed our lives. But not as much as the washing machine.

The fact was, houses needed wives (or servants). You couldn't throw your clothes on a spin cycle and forget about them, a laundry kettle needed constant attention and stirring, the clothes had to be plucked out by tongs and fed through a mangle. It was a dangerous operation of potential scalds and squashed fingers. It was also a hard day's labour. Automatic machines arrived in 1957 as Elvis was 'All Shook Up', but by 1970, as Simon and Garfunkel released 'Bridge Over Troubled Water', 35% of UK women were still elbow-deep in the laundry tub.

Bowie rang in the Ch-ch-ch-changes – a host of time-saving devices came into the home throughout the 1970s – freezers in the garage, microwaves in the kitchen and cling film around our leftovers. Once we had control of our ovaries and were no longer held hostage by clean sheets and fresh cooked meals, we could take on the world.

The clouds parted when Diana Ross's 'Ain't No Mountain High Enough' topped the charts in 1970, and a group of gutsy women from Dagenham won equal pay for equal work. Five years later, the Queen signed the Sex Discrimination Act into law as Queen became Number 1 for the first time confessing, 'Mama, I Killed a Man'.

Anyone would think that's what we were trying to do.

When we arrived in the workforce we were met by the natives – lances drawn.

Despite the hostility, a few of the career pioneers have done brilliantly in business and public life, remarkable women who have played a faultless game even on the slanted pitch with the sun in their eyes. These brave women forged the path for all women behind them and, without their sacrifices, we wouldn't see the feminised workforce we see today. Yet, after 30- to 40-year careers, they are still fighting battles in rooms where they are still alone. Like all of us, they've made their mistakes. But those women chose to fight and they knew they were playing a long game. They still are.

*'If there isn't a seat at the table, bring a fold-ing chair.'*

– Shirley Chisholm, 1968

In the UK, most of the early career pioneers started their careers under a female leader, Margaret Thatcher, who was one ball-breaking bitch. The traditional men of government and business were terrified that if she got the top job just four years after equal opportunity legislation, what other monsters were about to be unleashed?

### Diane Abbott

**Black politician Diane Abbott began her parliamentary career under a Thatcher-led Conservative government, and even though the job of Member of Parliament is unlike any other, her path and career has lessons for all of us as her hard-won fight represents some of the intense battles a lot of women have faced on their way up the ladder to the peak of their careers. As well as the battles we face now in the twenty-first century as midlife women with all our experience and expertise as we fight to be seen and heard.**

**Diane Abbott is a pioneer and heroine for many women of African descent, and clearly many white women in her constituency of Hackney North and Stoke Newington. She made history when she was elected as an MP on 11 June 1987, the first woman of African-Caribbean descent to ever hold that role. It is the very first thing that's said of her in any profile, and while it isn't important to her, she understands that it is for many people of African descent. As she told**

interviewer Kirsty Young in her 2008 appearance on the BBC's *Desert Island Discs*, 'I remember when I was first elected meeting an older West Indian woman … she said, "You know every time I see you on the television, I feel big." And you know there were lots of people at the time for whom to see somebody like themselves in parliament was very empowering.'

In 1983, out of 650 MPs there were only 23 women serving in parliament. In the year Diane took her seat only 41 women were elected to parliament. There were no MPs of African or Asian descent, male or female, so a lot of people didn't believe a Black working-class woman could be voted into parliament. In fact, a lot of people in Hackney didn't believe she *could* get elected. And in the darkest hours of the night, after campaigning hard all day, even Diane sometimes wondered if she could. So when she prevailed with 48.7% of the vote, she was, in her own words, 'In a daze for months afterwards.'

In recent years, Diane has been much maligned, but a quick examination of her career reveals a dedication to serving the British public and a multitude of achievements.

The child of a welder and a nurse, Diane, bright and hardworking, passed the 11+ and won a place at Harrow County Grammar School for Girls. And on the first day, she found she was the only girl of African descent there. She was probably the first Black girl to attend the school, and she tells a story that is familiar to many children of African descent. Shortly after arriving there, her teacher set an essay assignment for her class, and the following week the teacher gave out the marks for the assignment. She started at the top with the students who'd received the highest marks ending with the ones who'd got the lowest marks. Diane listened as she went down the list from A+ then A, then A- and she still hadn't heard her name and was really surprised because in primary school she never got a lower mark than an A. She listened as the teacher read out all the grades and all the names of all the other girls in her class and her name was not called. When the teacher was done Diane went to her afterwards. The teacher's desk was on a dais maybe six-inches high and as Diane stood there the teacher picked up her essay between her finger and thumb, looked down at her and said, 'Where did you copy this essay?', because she could not believe that this chubby, bespectacled, Black girl standing in front of her could have written that essay.

For the rest of that year, Diane didn't write to her full potential because she never wanted to be humiliated like that again and it wasn't until she was in the second year with a teacher who believed in her that she began to blossom again. This was not the only time this kind of thing happened to her during her time at Harrow County, but she began the process of growing the thick skin she was going to need as an African-Caribbean woman in Britain.

While at school, Diane met Michael Portillo, when they both appeared in a joint school production of *Romeo and Juliet*, though not in the title roles. Although they did later play Macduff and Lady Macduff. Michael was the Conservative Secretary of State for Social Services when Diane took her seat for Labour in 1987. The two went head to head on many occasions that year, and went on to be regulars doing the same on national television on the BBC's current affairs programme *This Week*.

Although none of her teachers thought Diane was Oxbridge material, Diane insisted she be given the opportunity to sit the exam. She proved she deserved the opportunity when she was accepted at Newnham College, Cambridge, where she studied history under Simon Schama. Ever the pioneer, when Diane Abbott attended Cambridge in the early 1970s she beat impossible odds to do so. She says it helped that she didn't know the odds were impossible. She was the only person of African descent in the history faculty. As recently as 2016, only 39 students of African descent were admitted to a Cambridge college, and 22 of them were male.

This was the first in a series of British establishment institutions she learnt to navigate and the experience taught her that she was as good as anyone else. As a woman of African descent that's a really important sense to have. It also helped Diane not to fear taking on seemingly impossible tasks at impossible odds – which may be why she was exactly the right person to be the first woman of colour to win a seat in the House of Commons.

After graduating with her history degree, Diane became an administrative trainee at the Home Office, part of an accelerated leadership development programme leading to senior positions in HM Civil Service. Between 1978 and 1987, she worked as a race relations officer at the National Council for Civil Liberties, as a researcher and reporter at Thames Television, a researcher and reporter at TV-am, a press officer at Greater London Council under Ken Livingstone and was head of press and public relations at Lambeth Council. In 1982, she was elected to Westminster Council, serving until 1986.

Diane has always been forthright about her ambition. 'My life has been a search for power, and every time I get to where it's supposed to be, I've been told it's just gone.' But unlike many men, Diane wasn't talking about personal power, but rather the power to create change. She believes you have to be where the leaders are so that you can use the power of democracy to persuade and effect societal change in order to make the world a better place.

As a Labour MP, Diane Abbott is often seen as a bit of a maverick within the party. She's a woman who acts in accordance with her conscience to push for the change she believes in. Her 2008 '42 Days' speech on civil liberties in the debate on the Counter-Terrorism Bill won *The Spectator* magazine's 'Parliamentary Speech of the Year'. Her work on this issue was also recognised at the Human Rights Awards and she received a special award jointly presented by JUSTICE, Liberty and the Law Society.

In 2010, Ed Miliband made her Shadow Minister for Public Health, with responsibility for a range of issues including children's health, sexual health and nursing. In 2011, the *Telegraph* said that Diane had become 'one of Labour's best front bench performers'. In January 2015, she was one of 16 MPs who signed a letter to Ed Miliband calling on the party to commit to oppose further austerity and was one of a tiny handful of MPs to defy the Labour Whip to vote against the Tory austerity cuts later the same year. She didn't just don her Wonder Woman amulets to go into battle for her constituents, she fought for all constituents in every constituency in the UK who were suffering because austerity was cutting services and the safety net from beneath them. Even those who don't like her, or agree with her politics.

And her constituents? They know she's in their corner and they show their trust and belief in her by returning her to parliament general election after general election. She entered parliament with 48.7% of the vote, but she's regularly returned with over 50%. In the last three general elections she received the support of 62.9% of voters in 2015, 75.1% in 2017, and 70.3% in 2019, making her constituency one of the Labour Party's safest seats.

Diane is not popular with everyone, however. In recent years, the rise of social media has seen the abuse that female MPs face rise exponentially. However, a statistic that should cause your hair to fall out in shock is that half of all abuse received by female MPs is received by Diane Abbott. It's hard to imagine the effect that kind of abuse has on a person. Even if people don't agree with Diane, there is no excuse for the kind of misogynistic and racist abuse she receives.

*As a midlife woman, Diane Abbott has much to teach us about resilience and perseverance.*

YOU HAVE TO BELIEVE IN YOURSELF.

Because you can't depend on anyone else to believe in you. There will be people who think you're mad, and will ask why, at your age, are you starting a business or a new career? Surely that's a younger woman's game? Don't even bother arguing with them. You don't have to prove yourself to anyone – not even yourself. Believing in yourself is giving yourself permission to make mistakes, to get knocked down and get back up again.

PERSEVERANCE IS THE KEY TO SUCCESS.

Diane's whole career has been about perseverance, from her single-minded service to her constituents, to ensuring that their needs are heard in parliament, her willingness to take the unpopular path, to saying the things that need to be said, as opposed to the sound bites. She wouldn't get such high voting numbers in her constituency if she wasn't working for everyone who lived there, not just the people who've voted for her.

RESILIENCE IS THE DAUGHTER OF PERSEVERANCE.

Resilience and perseverance are closely related. These qualities are really needed if you're setting up a business or changing career in midlife. Women like Diane show us that if we persevere and use the resilience that we each have, we can build something new in our midlife.

TRUST THAT YOU HAVE EVERYTHING YOU NEED.

Diane had many jobs that prepared her for what she considers the most important job in the country – barring being prime minister – being a midlife woman. And as one, know that all your experiences will come to bear in your new career or new business. You really do have everything that you need.

The early female career pioneers may have been painted as nemeses, but with time, justice will always prevail. Many women have hung in there to find great success, many more walked away. Back in the day, it seemed we only had two options. The patriarchal system set so many traps that the influx of ambitious women who arrived had no choice but to fight like mad or run like hell. That didn't feel right. And we were right.

We've all heard men who say women are a complete mystery to them or way too hard to understand. Now we've got the receipts:

When men had free rein over medical research, the thought of including female subjects in their clinical trials was considered a waste of their precious time. Our bodies were seen as 'too complex due to fluctuating hormones'.

Women weren't officially included in medical research until 1993. So seven years later, when scientists at UCLA discovered the 'fight or flight' reflex had only ever been tested on men and male mice, a new generation conducted the same experiments on women and female mice and a whole new reaction to stress was discovered: tend and befriend.

This is a natural physiological reaction that goes back to more primitive times. While the first men were running around the woods running from or fighting wild beasts, women found another way to protect the tribe.

It's perhaps best described by this 2018 tweet:

> I played Dungeons and Dragons with my daughters.
>
> They were supposed to fight the wolves surrounding a town.
>
> Instead, they fed the wolves and turned them into their friendly wolf army.
>
> Girls, man. They'll take over the world.

And it looks like they've already started. On 20 June 2020, the headline in the *New York Times* read, 'TikTok Teens Trash Trump Rally in Tulsa'. The powers that be had no idea of the power of a teenage girl's first popstar crush. Someone on TikTok did and took it one step further with an idea on how to humiliate the then most powerful man on the planet and showed teen K poppers how to reserve blocks of tickets to the rally. Trump boasted of his million ticket requests; 6,200 people turned up, less than one-third of the stadium's seating capacity, and the outdoor viewing areas were dismantled before the rally even got going. But far from the boys in their mums' basements that the world imagines internet chaos-mongers to be, in this instance the ringleader was . . . a 51-year old grandmother from Iowa.

No one saw her coming!

# 7

# INTERLOPERS

## *White women get to work*

December 2017

> DRUNK CLIENT
> So of all the girls in your year
> at school, how many left to take up
> 'careers'?

Jane thinks hard, counting her school friends
in her head.

> JANE
> Ooh not many, we were pretty much the
> first with that option ... I dunno, ten
> maybe fifteen?

> DRUNK CLIENT
> So you're the bitches that ruined
> everything.

One of the great gifts of midlife is the ability to control knee-
jerk reactions, somehow a pause, an internal eye roll and

quiet intake of breath can work wonders, but it takes years of practise. In my younger days, a provocation like the one above would have led to a disdainful feminist diatribe. My more mature mindset, however, was far more effective: I allowed him to elaborate. I realised if I put my feelings to one side, I could actually find out what was really going on behind the bluster. Apparently, if we'd just done what we were supposed to and ignored all that 'women's lib rubbish' everyone would be happier: men would still understand their role in society and women wouldn't feel a 'career' was compulsory.

Careers were anything but compulsory in our day. Each year more and more women joined the workforce in professions that had previously been just a pipedream. Each industry threw up a different set of challenges and many of our experiences were unique. I use my early career of entering advertising as an illustration. I was an interloper – which the dictionary describes as '*a person who intrudes into some region or field of trade without a proper licence*'. In the early days of career women, for 'proper licence' read 'penis'.

My first letter of employment as a junior art director in a hot new London agency was addressed to Jane Evans, Esq. I never knew if it was an old habit dying hard, an honest typo or the first of many digs from the creative department secretary. In the glamorous advertising industry, most secretaries were upper-class women (or Sloane Rangers as they were affectionately known back then) who had got the job through Daddy's connections to do a little typing while hunting for the most eligible man to marry. They did not know how to treat women as anything other than inferiors or competition, and had no clue how to handle an influx of young women who were cleverer, funnier and above them in the pecking order. The boys in our department could throw anything on the secretary's desk and it would be typed without question. I couldn't get anything typed without offering to donate a kidney.

It wasn't just the secretaries who were wary of us. We may have been the first women in the workplace with the legal right to be there, but there were a few brave souls who had built careers before us. They didn't have our sense of entitlement; most of them had become tougher than their male peers just to survive and saw us as, what we'd call today, 'diversity hires' and unnecessary competition. Which was particularly tough when there was only ever one space on the next rung of the career ladder. Agencies tended to have a few young women in their creative departments, but only one would be given the opportunity to go on to bigger and better things.

I had fewer problems with the pioneers before me partly because it was obvious I was going places, but also because I was blessed to work under and be mentored by two of these amazing women early in my career, female creative director Lyn Middlehurst and Barbara Nokes, a heroine to look up to, she is still considered one of the greatest female copywriters of all time. She was an uncompromising genius. To this day, many women who worked under her shudder at the mere mention of her name.

*'You can only sleep your way to the middle.'*

Barbara Nokes

The generation of women who entered the industry with absolutely no rights made sure we all knew what we had to do to earn our place. Of course, some women did use sex to get ahead, but nowhere near as many as most men thought. Yet they presumed we all were fair game. For most of us, work social events meant finding creative ways to avoid men with nicknames like 'Mr Sausage' or 'Sleaze Montgomery'. But honestly, it wasn't just the Christmas Party where we had to keep our backs to the wall. On my first-ever TV shoot, the client tried to grab my boob. Apparently, he thought I was part of his £250,000 production budget.

It wasn't all a fight. One group who welcomed us with open arms were the young men we worked alongside and competed against professionally. I'd found the same when I was the first girl in woodwork class at school. It wasn't till many years later I found out the boys were all so eager to help me catch up on six years of dovetails because of, well, boobs. My contemporaries at the ad agency saw me as a worthy opponent though and treated me as such. Yes, they drew cartoons of my arse and I have a collection of leaving cards and trade press clippings dedicated solely to my boobs, but for the most part it was good-natured, probably because the last thing we ever confessed to being was feminists. We were just 'one of the lads'. It was the only way we could get on. We laughed at their sexist jokes, tolerated their nicknames and cried in the bathroom every time they got an opportunity we could only dream of. Our bosses told us we worked in a meritocracy. And many believed them. Too many women left promising careers because they genuinely thought they weren't good enough when, in reality, they simply weren't male enough.

Somewhere along the way those friendly competitors made it to the top and turned out to be just as sexist as the men in business before them. Today they call us 'nasty' women, which is a major relief from being called bitches, witches, lesbians (like it was a bad thing), she-devils and my personal favourite, 'fucking hairy-legged fucking feminists'. I heard this, twelve years into my career, as one of the bosses loomed over me (which was unusual – I was six foot in heels – I always wore heels). He was flushed with anger, hissing and spitting and poking me in the chest ranting, 'If women want to play hardball, men will play even fucking harder.' What had I done to provoke such a violent reaction? I had casually asked how his radio interview on the positive portrayal of women had gone.

I was an ambitious and talented woman. I was certainly not a radical feminist. At the time it was every woman for herself, but I was fighting to get as high as I could so I could send the elevator back down. That encounter changed my life, I went from being a woman trying to succeed, to being perceived as the head of a terrorist organisation. A responsibility I was not prepared for. And a vicious battle I didn't expect.

I certainly didn't deserve a couple of months later to be handcuffed by police to a hospital gurney saying in my best Edina, 'But darling, I'm wearing Zampatti – one simply can't be committed in Zampatti.'

What really upset me about my first career knockout was that I didn't crack a joke till it was too late. I had cracked. I had failed the training that began before I even set foot in an ad agency.

Before computers and when photocopiers didn't have a zoom function, art directors and designers had to draw layouts by hand and the only tech we had to help us was a machine of torture called the Grant Enlarger. Basically it was a massive camera lens in a box that you hoisted up and down to trace your type or picture projected onto a glass plate. To achieve this, you stood on a box, leaned in and pulled a blackout curtain behind you. Most of my art school days and early career were spent with nothing but my arse on display. My bum was first pinched the first month into my advertising course. I was 18 years old. I swung my head out from behind the curtain and was shocked and embarrassed to discover it was my tutor. 'What did you do that for?' He laughed, took a puff on his ciggie and said, 'You're going to be one of the first girls in a creative department, this stuff will happen all the time. You've got to have an answer.' He clicked his fingers three times, 'Like that, like that, like that.' His constant and often hilarious attempts at sexual harassment from there on in was the most useful education I got at ad college.

When I tell this story to younger women they are horrified that constant groping was part of my training, but when I started ad college in 1980, anti-sexual harassment in the workplace legislation was still six years away, and full acceptance of it even further, if it's really come at all. It saddens women like me deeply that the same bloody battles we fought out in the open are still being faced today just under the unsightly glow of gaslight. Certain men still try to make you think we're imagining their misogyny, that we must be mad and, of course, it was all a joke. For me, they took it to extremes: I was seen as ungrateful, wasn't it enough that I had a job and earned three times as much as a secretary? Wasn't I satisfied with my white sports car, warehouse-style apartment and trophy cabinet? Why did I want the 'man's' job of creative director too? Why? Because I was better than most of them, worked harder and deserved it more than they did. And I certainly would have known what to say on a radio interview about the positive portrayal of women.

Two years after being strapped to that gurney, when I had won practically every award going, sat on the leading creative committee in the business, had successfully run the industry training school, set up an industry body for the promotion of female creatives and won my client's highest global accolade for a campaign that I had handled for nine months without a creative director above me, I applied for the vacant creative director role. The CEO laughed in my face. Laughed!

I'm not retelling this as some generational one-upmanship in the feminist struggle (I could fill the rest of the book with horror stories if that were the case). I use it as an illustration of how much we faced to get a foot in the door for every woman behind us. I know that advertising was one of the most competitive fields to enter so the price of entry was always going to be high. But not as high as my friend's final interview for a new airline to become an air hostess (as they were called back then). She told me proudly that the final twelve had to sleep with the founder before they got the gig. Women in print media had it a little easier so long as they didn't stray further than the woman's section, and many women in music, television, film and the financial markets still curl up in the foetal position at the mere mention of their early careers.

How did I survive? Because I put what I learnt at art school to good use. One night working late on a pitch, I was at the Grant Enlarger arse akimbo when the boss dry-humped me from behind. I swung my head round, sighed and said, 'Can you do that to John? You pay him more than me.' The next day my wonderful female creative director gave me a wry smile as she handed me the parity pay rise (which doubled my salary) she'd been nagging management for for months. I proved you could also not sleep your way to the middle.

Getting to the top, however, proved impossible. I first realised this as a woman who wanted kids fifteen years into my career. My creative partner, Jane Caro, and I were considered 'senior', which allowed us the freedom to openly call ourselves feminists. This made our office the first point of call for women who needed to vent. I will never forget Jane Ketelby, the most brilliant account woman I ever worked with, lips pursed, trying her hardest not to cry, hissing with rage, '*He told me to get my priorities straight.*' There was a big client who hated his family, this was not something imagined or whispered, he openly expressed it was the agency's job to provide him with an alibi for never being at home and regularly requested meetings at 7 p.m. so he didn't have to do bath time, read bedtime stories or listen to his 'insufferable' wife. Why was the account director so upset? Her boss wanted her to choose that prick over her son's seventh birthday party.

Whether I chose career or motherhood it didn't matter

anyway. Around the same time, Jane Caro and I sat across from the leading headhunter in town who was telling us the boys had decided there would never be a female creative director in Sydney and we should just forget about it. We had officially hit the glass ceiling. It wasn't till almost 20 years later when a few of us shared our old clippings we worked out why. In 1995 creative women dominated the Australian advertising award scene, even with 100% male juries. We had gone too far. We fled. Jane embarked on her magnificent media and writing career and is now Jane Caro AM. I started my own agency, and it seems the other senior women were 'disappeared' and the young women below us were back to being pinned down on all fours and having penises drawn on their face.

Senior creative women didn't reappear in Australian advertising in any numbers till around 2015 when an organisation called the 3% conference (along with the very real threat of serious class action lawsuits) caused the global advertising industry to do the right thing. And it obviously wasn't just an Antipodean phenomenon, in 2015, 3% of the US creative directors were women; today 29% hold the title, the 3% figure has only risen to 17% in the UK – the rest of the world is still even further behind.

As the old Virginia Slims ads used to say, 'You've come a long way, baby.' The ad women of every era say, 'Nowhere near far enough!'

# 8

# INSPIRATION

## *Black women fight to work*

July 2020

> CAROL
> How are you enjoying your new job?

> WOC TV EXEC
> It's brilliant. I haven't felt this
> relaxed for years.

> CAROL
> What's the difference?

> WOC TV EXEC
> I feel trusted.

> CAROL
> First time?

> WOC TV EXEC
> (nodding vigorously)
> First time.

                    CAROL
(Cheeky grin)
Any chance of a commission?

                  WOC TV EXEC
Show me what you've got.


*'If you don't understand the history of African American women, you don't understand the history of America.'*

– Toni Morrison


While white women of my generation in the UK were striding into professional jobs and meeting the kind of sexism nobody today wants to believe is true, women of African descent were fighting for some basic human rights.

These women, my predecessors, were driven by what they'd left behind in their homelands, and the dreams they carried in their hearts. Dreams that would improve not only their lives, but the lives of the families they'd left behind. These are the women who have inspired African and Caribbean women to push past how we have been perceived and smash the stereotypes of us to smithereens.

When the HMT *Empire Windrush* brought those who have become known as the *Windrush* Generation to UK in 1948, slavery had been abolished only 110 years before. And in the 110 years since the end of slavery nothing in the Caribbean had changed. Most of the jobs available were the same jobs that had been available during slavery: field work on the plantations; or housework as maids, washerwomen, cooks, seamstresses and childminders. Nothing that could raise us out of poverty. Though that never stopped us trying. Many women and their families worked hard to raise money so that women could train as teachers or nurses.

But even before the *Empire Windrush* set sail in 1948, women of African descent were finding ways to leave the Caribbean and travel to the UK. One stereotype buster, Una Marson, arrived in 1932. A publisher, editor, journalist, poet and playwright, she'd busted stereotypes before she left Jamaica, when after a stint as assistant editor at the *Jamaican Critic*, she decided to publish her own magazine. She became the first female editor in Jamaica when she started *The Cosmopolitan*, in 1928. Her articles not only encouraged women to join the workforce and become politically active, there were also articles about workers' rights, women's cultural status and feminist issues.

For many of today's midlife female Jamaican writers living in the UK, Una Marson is a key inspiration. She arrived bringing her play, *At What a Price*, which had a critically successful run at the Ward Theatre in Kingston, Jamaica, before showcasing at London's The Scala in 1934, again to critical acclaim. Her plays explored sexual politics in a patriarchal society and satirised colonial policy.

She lived in London over two time periods, 1932–1936 and 1938–1945. In the first period, the racism she suffered led to her joining the League of Coloured Peoples founded by her friend, Dr Harold Moody, a prominent Jamaican doctor living and practising in Peckham, south London. She was very active in the League, editing and writing poems and articles for their publication, *The Keys*. She was a delegate to the twelfth Congress of the International Alliance of Women for Suffrage and Legal Citizenship, and she wrote – articles, poetry, plays – that focused on the identity of Black women in Britain. She just didn't stop.

She went through a mental health crisis and returned to Jamaica in 1936 where, after a brief break, she threw herself back into the growing struggle for independence, gender politics and the place of women of African descent in that fight for freedom.

A few years later, Una returned to the UK, in 1939, and not long after her return, she got a job at the BBC as an assistant producer – for television.

There's a 1944 BBC newsreel with footage of two Black men, one a soldier, the other in civvies, with an elegant, fiercely intelligent-looking woman of African descent. That woman is Una Marson. She was the first producer of African descent on the BBC's payroll. The men were taking part in *Calling the West Indies*, a mixture of messages from serving men and women to their friends and families back home, music and uplifting tales. She produced it from 1943 until the end of the war.

As a writer and creator of drama programming for television, when I first heard about Una Marson, I felt so proud I walked on air for almost a month. And today, whenever I come up against an obstacle in my career, I remember that it could be harder. I could be working in a more overtly hostile environment.

Representation does matter, and not just for me as a woman of African descent, but for the forthcoming generations, too. As Jamaican–Indian woman Kamala Harris was sworn in as Vice-President of the United States of America in January 2021, making history, young African American girls looked up and saw themselves, young Indian American girls felt the same, and many young white girls looked up at her wide-eyed with awe. Each one of them felt that she represented them, the possibility of what they could be. And we can't be what we can't see.

Similarly, all women of Caribbean and African descent who enter the world of film, television, radio and theatre stand on Una Marson's shoulders. We can because she did. And there are plenty more women of African descent who broke through barriers and did extraordinary things for the times in which they lived. Women who inspired those who came after them to work hard, bust stereotypes and more importantly, dream big.

Una Marson left the BBC in 1945, three years before the HMT *Empire Windrush* arrived. When the call from Britain went out, African-Caribbean women and their families pooled every penny they could lay their hands on and answered the call for workers to help rebuild Britain. When they arrived what they found was back-breaking work made more difficult by the shock they experienced at the racism they encountered. It was not uncommon for Black women and their children to be spat at in the streets and on buses – or hit or kicked. Many described the experience as one that mirrored that of their mothers, grandmothers and great grandmothers going back over five centuries.

When women like my mother arrived in the UK in the mid-1950s, they were prepared to work hard – they'd done that all their lives. But after looking long and hard for jobs they ended up as un-unionised cleaners, canteen workers, laundry workers and chambermaids or in factories. Even when they arrived as qualified teachers, as Beryl Gilroy did from Guyana, the only work she could find was in a café or as a lady's maid; she even worked as a dishwasher at Joe Lyons and in a factory. Real talk, to find these menial jobs could take weeks, sometimes months. Some women spoke of walking from south to north London looking for work. And when they finally got a job, the working conditions were poor, to say the least. Add to this, other workers going on strike, protesting against working with them, the racist name calling and the petty acts designed to torment the workers of African descent or any worker of colour. These experiences were traumatic for the newcomers, but they learnt to fight back.

My mother was a brilliant seamstress. My grandmother had sent her to apprentice with the best dressmaker across three districts, and she'd learnt how to make clothes from patterns she'd learnt to make herself. Although there were many

garment factories around east London, it was not easy to get a
job. My mother's first job when she came to the UK was bottle
washing. That lasted three weeks before she and a few other
women of African descent were sacked. Her next job was in
a garment factory as a top presser. Traditionally, this was a
man's job because the top-pressing iron was very heavy and
wielding it for eight hours a day was thought to be something
a woman couldn't do. Ironic when you think that there was no
distinction between the male and female enslaved, as women
of African descent were expected to work as long and as hard
as the men when it came to working in the fields. She'd laugh
as she told the story of how she got that job, negotiated the
same wage as the other four top pressers, and she became the
highest paid woman in that factory. But her victory of earning
the same as the men didn't last very long. The unhappy men
threatened to leave if the owner didn't give them a pay rise.
That didn't stop her from becoming a valued worker.

My mother's dream for me was to have the choice to do,
and be, whatever I wanted. And as far as she, and many other
African-Caribbean parents were concerned, the route to
fulfilling that dream was: Education! Education! Education!
Three words which many of us heard growing up more than
any others. It was seen by my parents and their generation as
the only way out of poverty and a good education was also seen
as the best answer to racism.

Doctor, lawyer, teacher were the preferred professions most
often cited in my home. Teaching is still a very respected
profession in Africa and the Caribbean. In the 1950s and
1960s being a teacher for women was one of the highest professional callings she could have in the Caribbean. In 1969
two Caribbean women became the first two headteachers in
Britain within months of each other. The first was Yvonne
Connelly in January 1969. The second was Beryl Gilroy in
March of the same year.

Yvonne Connolly arrived in London from Jamaica in the early 1960s and worked her way up quickly, unlike Beryl Gilroy, who'd arrived in London in 1951 from Guyana to take up a place at University of London. When Beryl arrived, not only was she already a qualified teacher, she'd been teaching for six years, so thought that would help her get a job in a school. It didn't. But determination sits in the hearts of women of the *Windrush* Generation and after many jobs – one as a lady's maid – she got her first teaching job in 1953 in a poor Catholic school. She taught for a couple of years before she got married and, as was the case in the 1950s, as a married woman she had to give up work. She home-schooled her two children and continued to educate herself before returning to teaching in 1968, by which point Yvonne Connolly, among others, had helped change the professional environment for women so that they could both become headteachers within months of each other, Yvonne at Ring Cross School in Holloway, north London, and Beryl at Beckford Primary School in West Hampstead in north-west London.

They both had to deal with the racism of the community around them. Yvonne had to be escorted into the building by security guards on her first day. She faced threats to burn the school down and abuse from the teachers who worked under her. But in spite of this, both women's pioneer spirit saw them achieve much. Yvonne created the Caribbean Teachers' Association essentially for Caribbean teachers to support each other. She also worked on the pioneering multi-ethnic schools' inspectorate, becoming a senior inspector in Islington, north London, before retiring in 2001.

When Yvonne Connolly died at the end of January 2021, she left a lasting legacy for those of us who stand on her firm shoulders. May she rest in eternal power.

Beryl Gilroy took another path. She headed up Beckford Primary School until 1982 and turned to writing. Her first

book, *Black Teacher*, a memoir of her experiences, was published in 1976. She became a celebrated author of fiction and
non-fiction after she left teaching. Her early work looked at the
impact Britain had on the Caribbean family and her later work
examined African and Caribbean diaspora during the period
of slavery. She was reported as saying, 'I wrote to redefine
myself and put the record straight' – a sentiment that echoes
my all-time favourite author, the late, utterly brilliant Toni
Morrison. One of the early women writers of African descent
of the post-*Windrush* era, Beryl's work continued the work of
clearing a creative space for writers like me.

Information on the achievements of British women of
African descent is scarce, or not easy to find, especially historical information. So what we know of Black women who
walked into the pages of history is all the more precious for its
scarcity. One of the professions where we do – although only
*just* – have the benefit of first-hand testimony is those who were
in nursing.

One of the only professions women of African descent were
allowed to join with any ease, nursing was one of the first
where the incoming group of Caribbean *Windrush* women
made their mark, despite the obstacles they faced. Many of
that generation of women have spoken about a question they
were frequently asked, the consequences of which they learnt
about the hard way: 'Are you a pupil or a student?'

In the 1950s, the nursing profession, with its low wages and
unsocial hours, was not a career many white British women
were interested in pursuing, and the newly formed National
Health Service (NHS) was creaking at the seams. It needed
nurses and it needed them fast. The majority of nurses were
recruited from the Caribbean, making women of African
descent the backbone of the NHS. It is an irony not lost on
us that Enoch Powell MP, he of the 1968 virulent 'Rivers of
Blood' speech, went to Barbados just a few short years before

that speech to recruit nurses during his 1960 to 1963 stint as Minister for Health.

However, what many didn't know when they answered the call was that they were entering a two-tiered system. After taking the General Nursing Council exam in the Caribbean, those who passed should have trained as student nurses in the UK. Why is this important? Well, if you were a pupil nurse, it meant you'd be training as an SEN (State Enrolled Nurse) instead of the more respected student nurse, who trained as an SRN (State Registered Nurse,) the more prestigious and internationally recognised qualification. An SRN could work anywhere in the world, whereas an SEN could nurse only in the country where she trained. Most of the *Windrush* women only found out the difference when they got to England or, if they were lucky, they heard about it from other nurses from the Caribbean before they began the journey here, or when they got here, just before they had to report for duty.

This was a big deal because there was no career progression as an SEN nurse. You couldn't be promoted to ward sister or matron unless you retrained as an SRN. And as many Caribbean nurses discovered, it was very difficult to get the references they needed from reluctant ward sisters and matrons to do so. The latter not only held their careers in their hands, they also controlled the renewal of visas and work permits. To make matters worse, none of the Caribbean islands these women came from recognised SEN as a nursing qualification, which meant they couldn't go home, back to their children in many cases, and get work.

Many women felt tricked into undergoing SEN training especially as they had passed the General Nursing Council exam which entitled them to train as SRNs. But the rewards for those who overcame the many obstacles placed on their path are exemplified by early pioneers like Guyanese nurse Daphne Steele, who went on to become the first woman of

African descent to become matron in 1964 at St Winnifred's hospital in Ilkley, Yorkshire. A blue plaque commemorating and celebrating her contribution to nursing was unveiled in her honour, in October 2016, at the site of St James Hospital in Balham, south London, where she trained as an SRN.

The struggles of these Caribbean nurses in British hospitals and how they dealt with them laid the groundwork for a change in attitude towards people of African descent. Because of their hard work and fortitude in the face of institutional racism and individual racist attitudes and behaviour, white people began to question the prejudices and assumptions they had about us. Our fight also had the added benefit of enabling us to influence areas of work in which acquiescence and compliance had been the rule – like the health service. There had been a feeling that those who worked in the health service – at least the women who worked there – should be prepared to give up their lives because the jobs required self-sacrifice, putting the needs of the patient above their own. This notion was shattered in 1972, when ancillary workers in hospitals, consisting largely of women of African descent, went on strike. That strike showed for the first time that hospitals were not immune to industrial action, and that we Black women were not going to allow ourselves to be exploited and abused.

In all the professions where women of African heritage have busted stereotypes and burst through glass ceilings, we've climbed on the shoulders of women who came before us – even when we didn't know who they were. Even when they weren't in the professions we've chosen. Women of African heritage can now be found in almost every profession. Some still only make up a handful of women in those professions, but we are there and we are continuing to break down doors and beat paths through untrammelled ground or ones that had become overgrown again.

I have been inspired by every woman of African descent

who chose to dream big and work among people who did not think she was capable enough, women who changed the minds of many so the experiences in Britain of the following generations could be different.

When I think of what has been achieved by the *Windrush* Generation, I remember my grandmother, Doris Francis Richards. She was a farmer. With her five acres, she was an entrepreneur. She grew and roasted coffee and, what we from the Caribbean call 'ground produce' – the staples of life – which she sold at the market. She held onto those five acres even though the owner of the nearby plantation tried everything he could to steal them from her. Mama was a tough woman, mentally and physically. She had to be. A single woman with five children, she had to be prepared to protect herself and her children from men who circled like jancrow (a native Jamaican buzzard), waiting for a moment of weakness. But she had a reputation for stubbornness and a hair-trigger temper. And her weapon of choice was her head. She was famous in the district for head-butting and could take down any man who came onto her land with a mind to trick her out of it, or her crops. In fact, her brother, Papa Benji, often had to be called to pull her off men, a fact all the women in my family are proud of, because it gives us the strength to fight, although not physically, for what belongs to us, including our dignity.

We, her grandchildren, are spread all over the world now. And we know that if she hadn't fought there and used the proceeds from her labour to help get all but two of her children to Britain to what she thought was a better life, we couldn't be here reaping the benefits of the opportunities for which our parents fought for us and which we, in turn, have also done for our children.

Women like my grandmother and mother, Una Marson, May Tanner, Kofoworola Abeni Pratt, Yvonne Connolly, Beryl Gilroy and Margaret Busby – who created the publishing house Allison & Busby in 1967 – have provided the shoulders women of African descent stand on today, even if we don't all know who they are. Many of these women went on to have second and third careers at a time when it was almost impossible to have one. These women have inspired me and continue to inspire me today.

So, to paraphrase my opening quote, If you don't understand the history of women of African descent in Britain, you don't understand the history of Britain.

With much thanks to my African American inspiration, Toni Morrison.

# 9

# INTUITION

## *The world needs our wisdom and experience*

October 2020

> CAROL
>
> So tell me, just so I've got this, why
> did you ask me if I knew Verna when
> we first met?

> JANE
>
> It's like when I find a four-leaf
> clover, Something tells me there's
> something different, I bend down and I
> pick it out. My dad could do the same
> and so could my gran.

> CAROL
>
> So it's sort of pattern recognition
> mixed with intuition then.

> JANE
>
> Yeah, you'd go mad if you looked
> for four-leaf clovers all the time.

Something told me to ask you because
without you, me, my mum and Verna
we're missing the magical extra leaf.

Woman's intuition is the stuff of legend. We've all got stories about how we 'felt' something that turned out to be important. Can it be explained? Maybe not for younger women but for those of us with a few miles on the clock it's tangible and empirical. We have experienced so much that we notice when things come around again (started spotting the latest shoulder-pad fad?) In scientific terms, this is called pattern recognition and it's one of the most important skills required in today's world. (Actually it's been a major factor in our survival forever.)

Theoretical physicist Satoshi Watanabe defined a pattern as 'the opposite of chaos; it is an entity, vaguely defined, that could be given a name'.

Boy, do we need the opposite of chaos right now!

Decades of repetitive experience gives us the ability to see patterns that only time can produce. When you lay patterns on top of patterns and discover where they intersect, you see a whole new story. And your brain physically changes to accommodate this advanced information. As the brain ages, branch-like dendrites that receive information grow, making stronger connections between distant brain areas so we're better at detecting relationships between diverse sources of information, seeing the big picture and understanding the global implications of specific issues. In other words, we finally get to see the wood for the trees.

There is, however, a price to pay for these new-found super-powers: we find it harder to encode new information and it can take longer to retrieve some information. But isn't that what Google's for?

Our intuition is so fine-tuned, not just because of what we've seen or heard before, but what we've felt. We have first-hand experience that the circumstances and triggers of our hopes, joys and fears may be different but the feelings can be very similar. In our earlier lives, we felt we were stuck on a roller-coaster of random emotions caused by circumstance. Our new-found neural pathways allow us the gift of understanding paradoxes like fear has an identical physiological reaction to excitement. Now we know, when our heart rate increases and our palms get sweaty, we can choose to be afraid or to throw our arms into the air and enjoy the ride. At our age, we'll more likely choose the latter because, sadly, for most of us the 'worst that could possibly happen' already has.

And therein lays our greatest superpower. We're time travellers.

We viscerally remember every moment and every emotion – and can travel back to any of them in a nanosecond. We've lived through grief and terror, fear and loneliness, dashed hopes, broken dreams and disappointments. We've also experienced great love, satisfaction, joy, friendship, community and the uncanny way that (with a lot of hard work and focus) things almost always turn out for the best.

Connect the patterns with emotions and you get intuition.

Use your intuition to make decisions and you have wisdom.

Use all that for others and you find the greatest leadership quality required for a world facing challenging times: empathy.

But how do you explain such woolly concepts as intuition, pattern recognition, empathy and time travel:

By telling three stories that intersect through sheer coincidence or a divine pattern:

## Jane

When Verna Wilkins moved to the white bread Tory stronghold of Camberley, Surrey, in the mid-1970s, I looked out of

the window and thought Makeda herself had moved in next
door. I vividly remember the most beautiful woman I had
ever seen alighting from a Renault 4 in a beautifully tailored
woollen suit.

And my father looking over my shoulder muttering, 'There
go the property values.'

My mum and Verna didn't care for each other's husbands
much, probably because they spent the next twenty years or so
moaning about them over cups of tea.

Mum had never met a Black woman before and her only point
of reference was the TV show *Love Thy Neighbour*. Barbara really
did love her neighbour: they were both women out of place.
My mum was a socialite, beauty queen and a farmer's daughter
who had regularly appeared in the society magazine *Tatler*; she
was locked in the suburbs with a husband who was well down
the pecking order at the golf club. Verna came from a powerful
family in Grenada and ended up living in a suburban box under
grey skies. They were both queens stuck in a white middle-class
prison, raising kids in relationships that weren't ideal, in a town
filled with judgement. Their experiences may have been different, but they damned well knew how the other felt.

Mum was the classic 1960s housewife; Verna was studying
at the Open University. They always caught the bus to town
together: mum would come home with a basket full of groceries – Verna's would be filled with books. Mum and I fought
tooth and nail for many years; she struggled raising a rebel-
lious daughter who had no intention of marrying a nice young
officer from Sandhurst (we had moved to the area specifically
for this purpose).

From an early age, I didn't feel like I belonged in the family
I had been born into; if I hadn't been born at home, I would
have thought there had been a mix-up at the hospital. The
routine killed me, Monday was wash day and cold roast with
baked potatoes for tea; Tuesdays were ironing and chops;

Wednesday cleaning and sausage and mash; Thursday was Ladies Day at the golf club …

I hated the golf club.

Every single thing about it.

I hated that our whole family life was built around it and that was all these people ever talked about. But the thing I hated the most was the Ladies Section. To me it was a pit of toxic femininity ruled by bitches who gained their power from their husbands' worth. I hated that the women were only allowed to play once a week, that they weren't allowed in the men's bar and none of them made a peep about it.

Verna was also the first feminist my mum had ever met. She was younger and became an important bridge between a woman who only wanted her daughter to marry well and the daughter who wanted to change the world. Verna showed Barbara that women could change the world.

When I moved to Australia in 1987, Verna started her publishing business. In my phone calls home, Mum knew the last thing I wanted to hear was news from the golf club so our weekly catch-up was usually filled with Verna's news. When I came home for visits, I would spend hours next door poring over Verna's stunning book illustrations, listening to her stories, laughter and fight.

Mum passed away young. She was only 64. Verna was there every step of the way when everyone's hearts were breaking. But there was also strength and laughter and a little bit of revenge. Verna sat in the front row of Mum's funeral cheering me on as I gave the eulogy and told the mean girls from the golf club who my mum really was. They judged her as the marketing manager's wife who couldn't afford designer clothes and couldn't keep her husband. My father had cruelly left her when she was 58 years old and many of the bitches at the golf club dropped her too. I gave it to them with both barrels. None of them had been in the *Tatler*!

But it wasn't till a few years later that I learnt something I had always felt but couldn't explain. It was 2002 and I was going through a very messy separation from the father of my children. I ran my own agency and I couldn't cry in front of my staff and clients. I couldn't cry in front of my ex- or his mother, who was living with us upstairs from the business. I couldn't cry in front of my daughters, who were both under four. I needed some space. I needed to come home.

Sitting at Verna's kitchen table, she told me a story I had never heard before. One day my mum had sat at Verna's table and said, 'I've finally worked it out. Jane's not my daughter, she's yours.'

I had been wrong for all those years, I wasn't born into the wrong family, I was blessed to have two mums.

## Verna

Going into publishing was not on my to-do list. Originally, I was a college lecturer at a Technical College in Surrey. I taught English, focusing on business English for 16+ in further education.

What prompted my decision were two things. One was bringing up two boys close in age and then realising that none of the books I could buy in shops or get from the local library in Britain showed images of Black children, or reflected their lives at all. The second was being a lecturer in Surrey in a college.

The pupils I taught were 99% white and every year I'd have to go through exactly the same thing. The pupils would come into the classroom and I would be there in the front of the class, but they would always ask, 'So where's the lecturer then?' And I'd have to explain it was me. Every year! And I realised that these kids had learnt, at the time, that an English lecturer didn't look like me. That's what they'd learnt. What they were looking for was a white male or, at a push, a female member of staff.

None of my white colleagues had to have that fight to identify themselves as the lecturer before they even opened a book. It was shocking. On top of that, I had my own children, young children, in the same system that had produced these children who sat before me every year. And I realised that *my* children were reading the same books at school as these children had read in *their* schools. It made me think what was the impact of invisibility on my children of colour? When they reached 16, would I be invisible to them too?

So, I set out to find books with Black children in them but I couldn't find any here. I did get a few from my sisters in America. And when the boys were little, my husband and I did a lot of things with them because I'd seen the dangers of omission and what it does to children, Black and white. But I kept coming back to the importance of children seeing themselves in picture books and, as they got older, in their reading material. So, this invisibility was also at the back of my mind.

What was crucial to me in creating those first books was to give children of colour a sense of self and personal value. Because if they don't see themselves in all jobs and roles in the world, they tend to grow up thinking some jobs are not for them. And non-Black children will tend to grow up thinking there are jobs Black people can't do, roles they shouldn't expect to see us in. Because racism isn't something someone is born with, it's a learnt behaviour.

The most significant parts of my journey to becoming a publisher were the visits to schools. Because I was in the teaching business, I started looking at schools and talking to teachers and they were so accommodating and so wonderful. I sought their advice; I wanted to know if what I was doing would work in their classrooms. I wanted to know that inclusive books would work in white areas, in Black areas, in mixed areas. They were the ones that told me that universal themes were the best way to go. Because in 1987, when I established Tamarind Books, a lot of the publishers had begun to see the dearth of images and stories of children of colour and one or two things came up in the press that alerted them too. But instead of just publishing universal stories, what they did was publish books with issues in them. So, you'd find a book with a Black child and she'd have to overcome other people's racist behaviour. I remember someone sending me a book that dealt with name calling by having the Black child saying, 'sticks and stones will break my bones, but names will never hurt me'. And I thought, hang on a minute, I don't want to be giving Black children resources to deal with other children's racist, bad behaviour. What I wanted to do was show Black children living ordinary lives: going to visit grandparents, losing teeth and being visited by the tooth fairy, not always living their lives in response to other people's attitudes to them.

So, when I started getting publicity as a Black female publisher of children's books – and there were other Black publishers around but they were publishing adult books – I was asked what issues my books dealt with. I said I didn't deal with issues, I dealt with universal themes that all children experience. So, the universal themes were like birthdays, losing teeth, going to school for the first time and then the teachers told me that they need to deal with teaching concepts.

Teaching concepts in books for Nursery and Keystage One pupils are about teaching subjects like up, down, by, over, under. So for early years work, I concentrated on these kinds of concepts, creating stories that helped children, in a playful way, learn about what 'up' and 'down' mean, for example. I put those ideas into the stories I published and those books got picked up by the schools, which was key to the success I had.

The bookshops wouldn't buy my books for a long while. The times I went in and they said to me, 'Oh no, we don't need those books here. Maybe try somewhere else.' Because all the books had Black children on the cover. They'd look at the cover. They wouldn't even open the books, because they were so sure that because they didn't have Black children in their area or schools, they didn't need my books.

I once went on a trade mission to Vancouver,

Canada, and I took one of my sons with me. By then he must have been about 19 years old and he worked with me for a year. It was very interesting and he was very perceptive. I wanted him to learn the business. At one of the meetings we attended, it was suggested that we go to meet with a bookseller who specialised in supplying all the local schools in the area with picture books. So, we made an appointment, and we went to see her. When we got to her bookshop, it was enormous. It must have taken up one-half of a block and the whole window was a display of book covers and illustrations of *The Gruffalo* by Julia Donaldson. So, we went into the store and we spoke with her, and showed her our books with Black female giants, Black tooth fairies and other Black characters. Now the production of these books was top notch because we knew we had to make sure that no one could criticise the quality. So, we had top quality illustrations, top quality printing. And this lady was very complimentary. She said, 'These books are beautiful, and I love the idea that you're doing this.' She was really nice to us. And then at the end she said, 'You see the thing is, I'm afraid I won't be placing an order with you today, because the people in your books don't really look like the people I supply.' And I open my mouth and started to say, 'Yes, but ... ' and then my son, who was sitting next to me, put his foot on my foot and pressed down hard and I shut up. I'd brought him with me to teach him something and here he was schooling me.

I thanked her for listening to us and looking

at the books and we walked out into the cold Canadian winter. When we got outside, I was heartbroken. I'd thought the meeting had been going so well. As we walked away, my son and I, we had this conversation.

'Why did you step on my foot?'

And he said, 'Mum, I knew what you were going to say.'

To which I replied, 'Am I that predictable?'

His response was emphatic. 'Yes, Mum. I know you.'

'So what was I going to say?'

'You were going to say, "Oh? You have a lot of Gruffalos living around here have you?"'

I had to laugh, because he was so right.

I've been asked by many people over the years, 'Verna, weren't you afraid of getting into this risky industry? It's so cost intensive. It's so labour intensive. Weren't you scared?'

But I wasn't afraid. Not because I was cheeky, or bold or bright. I wasn't afraid because I didn't know what to be scared of. With 20/20 hindsight, if I knew then what I know now, I would have been terrified. But you know, there's a lot to be said for not knowing what to be scared of: it gave me the courage I needed to approach teachers, other publishers and anybody else who had some piece of knowledge I needed.

People in publishing are very nice people and I benefited many, many times from the kindness of strangers. One was a company called Child's Play International in Swindon, which was so supportive. I was lucky enough that the late Michael Twinn, the owner, offered to allow me to piggy-back some of my titles on their print run, which dropped the unit price per book right down. And he would have the books delivered to my garage, because I ran my business from my kitchen table for many, many years. People like Michael Twinn and Neil Burden, who took over after Michael passed on, and the teachers who so kindly shared their knowledge of what worked in primary school and early years settings were invaluable. Those are the people that made my success possible.

That success didn't come through orthodox methods. Remember, I was being told that the people in my books didn't look like the people the booksellers supplied. That meant we were forced to be innovative and inventive in selling and marketing our books. One of the market-places I went to was the Black Hair and Beauty Show, held annually at Alexandra Palace in north London. The first year, I sold dozens of books. The next and subsequent years, I sold thousands. And building on that, we started to print bro-chures, because when the Black mothers came to our stall they'd ask us for brochures to take back to their children's schools and the local librar-ies, and this is how the business grew. We went from school to school carried on the breaths of Black mothers.

One of the things that gave me the most pleasure was seeing and hearing young Black children's reactions when they saw the books, 'Mummy, look! That looks like me.' 'Oh look there's grandad!' 'Mum! Look at her hair! It's just like mine.'

We sometimes faced the accusation from mainstream publishers that our illustrations looked old-fashioned, because at that time their illustrations were more caricatures. But Black children had never seen themselves in books before. White children had come down from a tradition of classical illustrations and then loosened up. Lynn Willey was one of my illustrators because she could do Black features and Black hair. She could illustrate cornrows, not just put a big black blob on top of the child's head. So, when the children saw realistic pictures of themselves, they'd gasp with joy and surprise.

Throughout my career as a publisher, I did workshops in schools. One was called, 'What's in a book?', which demystified the process by which a book is made. First, I'd give them the finished product, one of my books: beautifully written, beautifully illustrated. They would look at it and pass it around the classroom. Then I'd tell them and this is how it started, and I'd hand them the original manuscript with all edit marks, the crossings out, the corrections. I'd also spoken to the illustrator and asked her if I could borrow her roughs, and using the manuscript and the illustrations I'd show them that some of the words had been crossed out in the manuscript because the illustrator had drawn a picture that told that part of the story so I didn't have to write that part.

At one particular workshop, I think it was in Ealing, there was a little Black girl in the class who didn't take her eyes off me the entire time. She was about 10. When I'd finished the workshop she came up to me and she stood very close to me and she said, 'Can I help you pack up?' And as we packed the books, manuscripts and illustrations away she said to me, 'Can I tell you something?' And after I'd said, of course, she said to me – and it puts a lump in my throat even now after all these years. She said, 'Do you know I've always wanted to be an author, but I didn't think I could really be one until I saw you today.' The impact of that moment was so powerful for me, and I was so touched. I put my arms around her and told her if that's what she wanted to do she should go for it, because she could do and be whatever she wanted.

There were a few books that really stood out for me. The first one was *Dave and the Tooth Fairy*. When I first started, I got some coverage in the newspapers for Tamarind Books. In the early 1990s, I was contacted by one of the big publishers wanting to give me a four-book contract, because they were aware that they didn't have any writers of colour on their books. I was really pleased because they were offering a very nice advance, and all I had to do was send the manuscript in for the first book. And I wrote *Dave and the Tooth Fairy* and sent it in to them before the contract had been signed, and I said, 'Here you are. Now before we sign the contract is this the kind of thing you're looking for?' The editor looked at it and she said, 'Love it! Love it! Love it! But you cannot have dentures in a children's picture book, so you'll have to take that out. And there are no white characters in the book from the look of it. Who are the white characters? Because the Tooth

Fairy's Black; Dave's lost his teeth, and he's Black; his grandfather, well he's Black too.' And I replied, 'Yes, they're all Black. Yes.'

I was slightly amused at her bewilderment at what looked to her like I was ignoring white people, and that was bad. The fact that there had been no Black children in British picture books for over a century didn't seem to cross her mind. So, I said, 'Okay. Would you mind if I don't sign that contract and can you send the manuscript back to me, please, because I don't think this is going to work.' I lost quite a lot of money, which I needed, but what I knew was that I didn't have the privilege of taking out all the Black people from my story. So, I published it under Tamarind and we sold tens of thousands of books. It even won a Book of the Year Award. It was on the National Curriculum reading list for Keystage One for three years. It was Malorie Blackman's *Desert Island Discs* book.

A book that was both painful but satisfying to write was *The Life of Stephen Lawrence*.

Baroness Lawrence specifically asked me to write her son's story. Everybody wrote about his death and the circumstances of his death, but I thought it was as important to write about his life. What he was like as a little boy. What he loved doing. His hopes and dreams. That book also did well, and the reason it pleased me was that it told his story.

When I became a publisher I opened a door to the world of publishing to myself and I opened a door into the world where Black children could see themselves represented. So while publishing

**hadn't really been in my plans, not only has it given me great pleasure, it has been an adventure I wouldn't have missed for the world.'**

## Carol

I met Verna 2004/05. I'd been invited to a dinner where I would be one of half a dozen writers hand-picked by the wonderful librarian, storyteller and writer Sandra Agard. I knew Sandra because she had booked me as a traditional West African and Caribbean storyteller for Southwark libraries on many occasions and I'd also been the dramaturg, which is like being an editor and sounding board, for her play, commissioned by Talawa theatre company. Sandra had decided that us women writers of African descent should meet up – she knew us all because she'd booked all of us at one time or another to appear at Peckham Library.

We were due to meet at the Caribbean restaurant Cottons and I was running late. Luck was with me though; I found a parking meter really near to the restaurant and ran into the restaurant, my mouth full of 'sorrys'. I was pulled up short at the sight of two women I knew of, but had never met – Malorie Blackman and Verna Wilkins. Verna had flung her head back and was mid-laugh when I screeched to a halt at the table, jaw sweeping the floor. And this was before I'd met any of the other talented women at the table.

Malorie welcomed me, but it was Verna who patted the chair beside her and said, 'Come and sit down here by me.' I didn't have to be asked twice. I'd bought Verna's books for my nephews and niece, for my little cousins – in fact, for any small child that came into my life. Verna had created something that hadn't been there before – books for British children of African descent. Before Verna the Publisher stepped into a yawning chasm I had to go all the way to America to find such books and toys. Now here I was sitting beside her in a Caribbean restaurant surrounded by other authors of African descent. I thought I'd died and gone to heaven.

I'd seen Verna's books in the schools I went into as an African and Caribbean storyteller, and every time I saw them I felt proud. I recommended the books of all my author sisters to the children and young people I worked with, but Verna's books were important because they were books PUBLISHED by a publisher of African descent. Each book we bought allowed Verna to publish another, and that was important to me – even before I met her.

During a lull in the conversation, I looked around the table at the wonderful women authors: Catherine Johnson, Ros Stanley, Millie Murray, Valerie Bloom, Malorie Blackman, Sandra Agard. They're not all with us now – Ros, I raise both hands to you and bow low to your memory – but on that day I experienced a fierce pride that we were there, sat around a table in a 'club' that wasn't very large. I can't lie. At the time I didn't know why I was there; I even wondered if it was a mistake. Then Verna and Sandra said a version to me of, 'Before there was the book, there was the word. And sister, there are very few who can paint pictures with those words like you.'

I was humbled.

We'd meet at least once a year after that to share stories about our journey through the world of books, and in my case, theatre, folktales and television. We'd laugh, sometimes we'd cry, but I always left those meetings with a glow, revitalised and ready to take on the world.

It went deeper with Verna. I would call her from time to time. Ask her advice, knowing that she was giving me her hard-won wisdom. She is always generous with her time.

Watching her navigate an industry that we'd been locked out of for so long was like watching a queen. I watched her grit her teeth, bite her tongue and live to fight another day. She was regal. She was gracious. She was tough when she needed to be, but she always had time for anyone who wanted to learn. I stand on her shoulders knowing I can because she did. She is like my big sister.

So when Jane and I sat having lunch in 2014 in NFTS and she asked the question that would normally make me roll my eyes all the way up into my head that began, 'Do you know ...?' ending with 'Verna Wilkins', I had to laugh – I'd been getting ready to put poor Jane on blast. In that moment, I knew as much as I'd liked Jane before she asked that question, if she knew Verna, we were in this for the long haul.

Nobody knows why the universe sat Barbara's daughter next to Verna's friend in 2014, but somehow in a country of sixty-six million people two souls with a story to tell found each other. We never imagined we would ever write a book together; we'd always seen both of us in fabulous frocks gracing the red carpet at each other's premieres. But when we look at the places we met before we even met we know we're exactly where we are supposed to be – carrying on a conversation that started over 45 years ago.

We should all take some time to look at where we are, how we got here and how our connections are made – sometimes that acknowledgement, that recognition takes us in fabulous new directions.

# 10

# INDIVISIBLE

## *When wise women come together, we all come together*

November 2019

> CAROL
>
> How did your 'You ungrateful mother-fuckers' speech go?

> JANE
>
> They took the telling off for ignoring midlife women better than I expected. Four young women came up afterwards. Two said I'd made them cry, one praised me for calling out younger women for being bad sisters.

> CAROL
>
> Really?

> JANE
>
> And the fourth said my speech had her in bits. Her mum ended up living in her car. She thought it was just her.

This book is written as a positive affirmation for all midlife women. But we can't hide from the fact we have a lot of work to do to capitalise on our strengths and value. Currently we're just not employed at the level or pay grade we deserve, if we're employed at all. Too many career pioneers, somewhere between ages 45 and 48 (30 to 35 in tech), are the first to go in rounds of redundancies, followed by years of applying for jobs we have no chance of getting. Younger women have silently watched this happen over and over again and then have the gall to complain they don't have role models. And younger HR execs just turn a blind eye to our job applications as if career women never existed or they themselves will never age.

A few years ago, we were furious when young women claimed feminism was unnecessary: it was as if we fought for nothing. Fortunately that fad has passed, young women now proudly proclaim their feminist credentials. But what does it mean to them? Is feminism something to be proud of? Have we ever truly been good sisters?

One of the greatest tricks the patriarchy ever pulled was convincing women we were in competition with each other. We all grew up in uncharted territory and a lot of us fell for the patriarchy's greatest illusion, '*Women compete with each other to attract men.*' This may still be true on *Love Island*, in nightclubs or on Tinder, but it's a dangerous idea in the workplace and motherhood.

When white middle-class women first hit the workforce, this created a whole new battleground. Career women were seen by homemakers as radical and unnatural: if they were mothers, they were abusing their kids by not being there. Second-wave feminists saw homemakers as prisoners and traitors to progress. And it's not over yet. The United States still does not have equal rights for women written into its constitution. The Equal Rights Amendment, which was first tabled in the 1970s, was, in reality, stopped by male politicians, insurance companies and lobbyists, but it was blamed on a small group of white middle-class housewives who thought their 'privileges' were being taken away. These women would never accept a female president in their lifetime. Their leader Phyllis Schlafly published her last book on the day she died entitled, *The Conservative Case for Trump.*

And the irony of ironies is, though we don't agree for a single second with any of Phyllis's beliefs, she was a career woman and with her vast knowledge and brilliant debate skills she would have made a great Republican president!

In the UK, equal opportunity legislation came out in the mid-1970s when many of us had already chosen our path in life. The few of us who chose the possibility of a career were frowned on by those who'd already decided (or had no other choice) to take a nice safe job till they got married and popped out a kid or two. And that wasn't such a bad option. When we were born, divorce was almost unheard of and women weren't actually allowed to work in many careers once married. Marital bliss was a secure path and most of the girls we went to school with ended up as secretaries, hairdressers, air hostesses or nurses till Mr Right came along.

Then it all went wrong. Almost half of them ended up divorced and a quarter of them became single mothers. With no recent work history, the jobs they hoped to find when they exited their careers as mothers simply don't exist. In Australia, women over 55s are the fastest-growing group of homeless. It's not just career women who face invisibility. The world turns a blind eye to mums living in cars.

It seems no matter whether you chose full-time motherhood or a full-time career, there was only one choice that guaranteed a happy life – finding a good mate. Half of midlife women (whether career women or stay at home mums) have found a life partner who supports them, loves them and respects them. They are generally wealthy, satisfied and secure. It hasn't been all plain sailing and they work hard on their relationships, probably supported by girlfriends who've tried just as hard and failed.

These women know how lucky they are and how tough it's been for the rest of us. But we'd all agree it's a doddle compared to giving birth in the fields.

Sadly, many women of our generation have been damned for their choices, whatever their choices. Those who chose a career never had private pension plans or maternity leave when they needed them. And for 71% of UK divorcees, pensions were never even mentioned by their lawyers. Which means half of us don't have enough money to last the rest of our lives. And a terrifying amount of us don't have any savings at all.

What the patriarchy has done to us is a crime. But we don't have to be victims.

We can moan that we have to work longer. Or we can rejoice in the fact that we're living longer. Yes, it would be nice to slow down for a while, but 30, 40, 50 years? If you haven't got this far in life without realising that change happens, you really haven't lived! So let's give up our entitlement, however valid, and get real.

Let's not wallow in 'should've beens' and start looking for something meaningful and profitable to do. In the same way we've adapted to every curve ball life has thrown at us, let's evolve and give the world something it's never had before: wise women working together and supporting each other's choices.

*'Sisterhood empowers women by respecting,*
*protecting, encouraging, and loving us.'*

– bell hooks

It seems even the most ardent feminists have forgotten the words and inspiration from the wise women of our age. White women read Naomi Wolf's *The Beauty Myth* yet still spend a ridiculous amount on anti-ageing products. And the '*women who run with the wolves*' have allowed ourselves to be portrayed like every generation of older women before us as 'women sitting at home with cats'.

And no, we didn't read Sheryl Sandberg. There was no way we were going to '*lean in*'. We were long gone. But the job's not finished and our voice is missing. We need to get over our '*fear of flying*' and start fighting '*fire with fire*' again.

The patriarchy is still playing its dirty tricks. And even we are falling for them.

How infuriated do we get when we see our daughters facing objectification, harassment and outright sexism, yet worry our sons might not automatically become the kings of the jungle? We get annoyed when the world criticises young people for not fitting into the workplace, especially when they blame it on how we raised them. Yet we stay silent, instead of challenging business to become the environments we prepared our kids for.

The women, who fought for radical things like maternity leave, sexual harassment legislation and equal opportunities, have become silent. No wonder we're invisible.

And if the world we thought should be here by now isn't anywhere close, it's time to strap on the armour and head back into battle.

We've got to walk the walk and talk the talk again. There's a whole new world to pioneer.

The second half of our lives.

Let's start by agreeing we may not all call ourselves feminists even when we pretty much all agree with the principles. Because whatever we have called ourselves or the choices we made, we doubt there is an older woman on this planet who doesn't value her sisters. It is the women in our lives that bring the most support. The shoulders we cry on, the hearts who share our loves and losses and the feet that give us a kick up the backside when we need it.

The sisterhood has power. But feminism has baggage. Starting with the word itself.

When feminism got its name, the leaders of the suffragettes were educated upper-class white women. The first mass petition in 1866 was signed by women from many different social classes, including dressmakers, shopkeepers and blacksmiths' wives. But when it came to action, working-class women were punished more harshly. However well-meaning, feminism has never truly provided equality and it's certainly not an inclusive term: there are currently something like 19 different feminist movements and ideologies.

If you were building a movement for the twenty-first century you wouldn't use a wishy-washy definition as your name. Throw the word 'femininity' into a thesaurus and words like, gentleness, delicacy and docility come up. Admirable traits for well-to-do women of the Victorian era who coined the phrase. Femininity is an indulgence only afforded to those who don't have to get their hands dirty. There's nothing feminine about hard work. Simply by its name, feminism excludes many women of colour, working-class women, androgynous, butch and some trans women.

A lot of Black women have little time for it. They see it as an exclusively middle-class white women's movement. And who can blame them? In the early days, young African American women were forcibly sterilised if they had an illegitimate child. This wasn't considered part of the feminist agenda. Their lower wages and poor living conditions weren't considered a priority either. Women of colour were supposed to take one for the team and sacrifice their rights to get white women in the boardroom, then wait for the new white female saviours who, of course, never came. In 2019, all 25 female executive directors working for FTSE 100 companies were white, as are 97% of the female executive directors of FTSE 250.

When Black women walked away from second-wave, middle-class, white feminism, they created a whole new movement with a powerful name.

*Womanism.*

African American author and poet Alice Walker first used the term in 1979. She defined a 'womanist' as a Black feminist or feminist of colour. The word comes from a common expression, 'You acting womanish', used by Black women to describe young girls acting beyond their years. As Alice Walker says:

'The womanish girl exhibits willful, courageous, and outrageous behavior that is considered to be beyond the scope of societal norms.' That's a pretty sassy word to describe a movement. But there's so much more at the heart of her words:

> A woman who loves other women, sexually and/or nonsexually.
>
> Appreciates and prefers women's culture, women's emotional flexibility ... and women's strength ...
>
> Committed to survival and wholeness of entire people, male and female.
>
> Not a separatist, except periodically, for health.
>
> Loves music. Loves dance. Loves the moon. Loves the Spirit
>
> Loves struggle. Loves the folk. Loves herself. Regardless.
>
> Womanist is to feminist as purple is to lavender.

No matter what sort of feminist you are, if at all, wouldn't it be great if us wise women could work to put all our differing shades of belief together to make the deepest, most powerful, shade of purple. The colour of queens.

We should fall in behind and marvel at how Black women

have never lost sight of their sovereignty. White women should acknowledge and make amends for the well-intentioned but exclusionary path the feminism movement took and we can start by calling ourselves the only term that describes all of us:

*Women.*

Because language is important, especially when we describe ourselves. So why the hell do grown women call themselves 'girls'? We do ourselves a massive disservice when we infantilise women. It's another of the myriad reasons why only younger women are valued and older women disappear. If we want to be taken more seriously and have long careers, we should think about practising more professionalism by objecting to inappropriate use of the word 'girl' in the workplace. Once we pass 18, we are grown-ass women and we should respect ourselves as such.

Because words are power.

'Woman Power' has far more depth than 'Girl Power'.

Being a 'handsome woman' has more substance than being 'pretty'.

And being a crone has always been the most exalted position of all, the patriarchy's silly tales turning the word that means the 'Crowned One' into an ugly old woman who hides in the woods.

It's time to straighten our crowns, Queens. We've got a world to change. Together.

# 11

# INCOMMUNICADO

## *Time for a cuppa*

As women who grew up without mobile phones, computers or the internet, we marvel at the connections technology has given us. We love social media – almost 300 million midlife women are currently on Facebook. Video calls were the stuff of science fiction to our younger selves: now we FaceTime, WhatsApp and Zoom with abandon. But there is a dark side.

When Google, Facebook, Twitter, et al., launched, no one really understood how they made money. In the beginning, it seemed they were creating these really useful platforms without any advertising revenue. Turned out they didn't need it. They were gathering something of far greater value – our data.

The social media giants know everywhere we go, everything we search for (including what we delete). They have our photos, our friend lists; they know everything we've clicked on and where we sit on the political divide. And they sell it to the highest bidder. The Cambridge Analytica scandal highlighted that the data on 87 million Facebook users was used to develop 'psychographic' profiles of people in order to deliver leading (and often misleading) messaging to sway people's political beliefs and votes. This has led to social media factories in Russia filled with brilliant, creative, English-speaking, digital natives who make silly memes to feed us dopamine and lies.

We've shared misinformation left and right. We seem to have made outrage our default setting and reduced arguments to a single point and perspective. We're judging on sound bites and sharing snippets. Short cuts and ill-informed memes have got us addicted to instant gratification and we're shouting people down before they've had a chance to speak. We can't ask questions without being labelled and there's no such thing as the middle ground anymore. If you don't agree with everything someone says you agree with nothing. This is ridiculous. What's worse is; we're led to believe this is all coming from our friends. It's not.

Let's get offline, grab a cuppa and find some truth.

Social media is not socialising – sitting down and talking is. No one ever meets a friend and immediately starts ranting about politics or religion; in fact many of us were raised that such things weren't brought up in polite conversation. When you actually meet, conversations don't start with our differences; they always begin with what we have in common and showing care for each other. 'How are the kids?', 'Did Alli get that job?', 'What's Brian done this time?'

Ask yourself, when you met with friends prior to five years ago, was Britain's role in the EU a regular conversation piece? Did we chat endlessly about US politics? Or care how bendy our bananas were? Of course, we didn't. And it's not embarrassing to admit we're being swayed by social media – we all are. We now have to be wise about how we use it.

Let's start by organising a get-together (online or off) with our womenfolk and communicate like grown-ass women about the people and the issues we really care about and the things we can actually do something about. Let's be open and honest, if we're struggling let's help each other, if we're doing well let's give those who are not a hand. Let's throw around ideas, pool our resources, mine our networks and make cunning plans. Let's not kid ourselves that we'll always be in accord with each other, but let's rejoice in the fact we're old enough and wise enough to recognise when it's best to agree to disagree. Because when we brush aside the small stuff and chat about our shared experience there's nothing more powerful than a whisper network. #MeToo hit the newsstands in 2016, but it was whispered first on MySpace ten years before by sexual abuse survivor Tarana Burk. The news of Harvey Weinstein's sexual violence was nothing new to any woman who entered the film industry; even at film schools it was whispered never to be alone in a room with him.

We don't always have to fight something. The same networks can inject some real optimism into our lives. Instead of moaning about all the things that are wrong in the world and out of our control let's see what actions we can take as a group, no matter how micro those actions or that group may seem.

Then grow that group – this is where the power of social media really lies. Contact that LinkedIn connection whose posts you always like, that Facebook friend of a friend that has a dog like yours or that person on Twitter who always makes you laugh. Don't be shy. If you know what it feels like to be invisible you can rest assured a DM out of the blue to a midlife woman is either a delightful surprise or a delicious intrigue. It's time to invite women you've only typed to for a Typhoo.

Or someone you haven't seen forever. Who better to have a chinwag with about the benefits of ageing than the girls you grew up with? Or discuss empty nesting with your old mother's group? We can easily write a whole new story for midlife women when all we have to do is catch up with old friends, old enemies, past acquaintances and marvel at how much we have all grown and make a whole batch of new friends who we can grow with.

Because in a world that is struggling to find some real truth, we all know that a pot of tea makes everything just that little bit better.

# 12

# INTERMEDIATE

## *It's not just young and old – there's a whole new middle*

September 2019

> JANE
>
> You are not going to believe this one.

> CAROL
>
> Go on.

> JANE
>
> Apparently the reason there are no older people in creative departments is because we represent death.

> CAROL
>
> What the actual?

> JANE
>
> When the young see our wrinkles it reminds them of their own mortality. I know. I had a very nice man explain it all to me.

Oscar Wilde famously said, 'Youth is wasted on the young.' A concept that had far more urgency 120 years ago. Oscar died at the tender age of 46. It seems such a tragedy to lose someone so young. Or was he old? For a man of his time, he was only one year shy of his life expectancy. At the start of the twentieth century, midlife lay somewhere between 20 and 30 years old. These days, we're lucky if our kids have left home by then!

Many of us joke, we've been midlife forever. When we were in our mid-thirties, we were expected to live till 70, now some are saying healthy boomers could live to 120, so a hell of a lot of us haven't even reached the middle yet.

Sometimes it's hard to imagine just how fast the world changes and how quickly we are learning and evolving as humans. When Mr Wilde left this mortal coil, there was no such thing as a radio receiver or even a bra. Back then, the sum total of human knowledge doubled approximately every 100 years. By the end of the Second World War, it was doubling every 25. Today it's every 13 months and in a couple of years when the Internet of Things is connected to and connects with everything from our fridges to our driverless cars, our knowledge will double every twelve hours.

The world is about to see a technological revolution on a scale never experienced before.

One thing's for sure: it will bring biological, mechanical and health innovations that will lead to longer and healthier lives and if we don't change the world's perceptions of midlife women now, we face being locked out of a bright future. Or worse, a world where nothing really changes.

We're on the cusp of a major technological and social revolution. We need all voices, all experience, and all imaginations to create and navigate this new world. If we follow the lead of the agricultural, industrial and digital revolutions, which were created mainly by white men, then nothing will really change.

Replacing old white men with young white men won't cut it either.

In 2007, Mark Zuckerberg, who was all of 23 years old at the time, stated with all the arrogance of youth, 'Young people are just smarter.' Which is ironic when he built Facebook as a 'hot or not' ranking system that would drastically alter an older, wiser man's far-reaching vision – the World Wide Web.

Tim Berners-Lee envisioned that his creation could, in the wrong hands, become a destroyer of worlds. In a 2018 *Vanity Fair* interview, he said: 'We demonstrated that the Web had failed instead of served humanity, as it was supposed to have done, and failed in many places. The increasing centralization of the Web has ended up producing – with no deliberate action of the people who designed the platform – a large-scale emergent phenomenon which is anti-human.'

There can be no doubt that the future is going to see machines and automation change the face of the world. Covid-19 has speeded up this process and thrown it into chaos. It's time for big thinking and rapid action. It's a golden opportunity to see where we can improve as the human race and alter our course.

Once the hard labour and repetitive tasks are taken care of, our greatest skill will be our humanity, and midlife women have that in spades. Young people may be smart, but there is no shortcut to wisdom. Wisdom comes by learning from a lot of mistakes. And putting things right. In his 60s, Tim is leading the charge to redesign and redefine his world-changing invention to benefit us all. In 1989, foresight could not warn him that the internet would create behemoth social media giants, but 20/20 hindsight can give him answers and new tech will allow him (or someone just like him) to build something just as wonderful and valuable, where we own and profit from our data and control how it's used.

It's not just the internet that needs changing, we have a

whole world to put right. The belief that 'young people are smarter' and the myth that 'digital natives' are superior are dangerous ideas and the last pathetic shot from the patriarchy. If they can't divide us by gender they can divide us by age. Or as they like to call it – demographics.

Demographics are a relatively new weapon and, like most of the best patriarchal propaganda tools, came from advertising. After the Second World War, advertising was seen as one of the few jobs openly available for women. As the 1947 *Girl's Companion's Career Guide* explains:

ADVERTISING

The advertising field offers variety and scope to those considering a business career, and who have the necessary self-confidence and initiative. Those who write good English and have a flair for words may specialise as copywriters, or you may specialise in layout – the most striking methods of presenting an advertisement. Some secretarial training is advisable, followed by a practical course at a training school. But the actual experience is the best training here, and as soon as possible a post in some advertising office or department should be secured.

When the *Girl's Companion* was published, women had just finished running the country while the lads were fighting the war – many had a taste of a career life and liked it. After the Second World War, the women who manned the advertising agencies were given a new mission – to conscript working women back to the kitchen. They used their brilliant wordsmithing to create a new enemy to vanquish with a name, previously pretty much only used by virologists and scientists, that sounded eerily like the old enemy – germs.

The brief was simple and the target market defined – the

women who actually bought the products. The ads were written by people who not only understood the target market – they were the target market. Then along came TV advertising and there was a lot of money to be made and fun to be had. What had been seen as a middling career creating radio and print ads was now a licence to print money. It became cool to be an ad man. The women in creative departments were rapidly replaced by the mad men.

Instead of using the insight and intuition of brilliant women to talk to other women, the new agency model created 'planning' which divided us up into demographics of gender, social class and age, planners researched for insights to try and understand us. This research was based on groups of women, usually middle class, always white and almost always a group of friends, who met to discuss their opinions on the latest product or ad over tea and sandwiches for an envelope filled with pin money. As you can imagine, stereotypes abounded and little insight was gained. But that really didn't matter.

At the time, there were only a few commercial TV channels, mass communication was the only way of reaching your market so everything was aimed at the lowest common denominator. A whole generation of very different women were defined by class and age bracket with communications aimed at them written by people whose only understanding of womanhood was based on their wives, mothers and sexual fantasies.

Then Billy Idol came along with his pretty-boy pop punk and made things even worse. He coined the phrase Generation X in the 1970s and, sadly for humanity, it stuck. The planners latched onto the name to lump millions of people into one big generational box. And it didn't stop there.

Gen X led to Gen Y, more often referred to now as Millennials. And now there's Gen Z.

Billions of people are now packed to the rafters in bizarre pigeonholes with labels that say:

Boomers are greedy.
Gen X sits on their arses.
Millennials are entitled.
And Gen Z needs emotional support.

Of course, it's all total bollocks.

We all know young people who are wise beyond their years and 50-year-olds with the imaginative powers of a child; we know 25-year-olds who could run the world and 80-year-olds who could run a marathon. There always have, and always will be fast starters and late bloomers. The beautiful thing about this world is it's filled with amazing people. Beautifully different people. By generalising whole generations we miss out on the gifts each brings. Everyone loves the excitement and creativity of the digital natives but the Boomers and Gen X were there for the birth of tech. We know how much it changes the world – we've experienced it first-hand.

We also know what we could be in danger of losing. Digital natives who never experienced the impact tech had on the analogue world don't see the irony that they all seem to have vinyl record collections. Those of us who saved our pocket money for the Beatles' *White Album*, Bowie's *Ziggy Stardust* or Wonder's *Songs in the Key of Life* totally understand. We pored over the artwork, read the lyrics till they were ingrained in our memory and played both sides till the needle broke. We loved shiny things, too. We replaced our records with CDs, then we transferred them all to our iPods. That's when we lost our prized collection and our precious art. We've lost the album too and the stories they tell. We now stream singles instead of experiencing a stream of consciousness.

We all have something to contribute and we can easily

dismantle the generational divide by looking through the lens of longer lives. When Oscar Wilde was alive, there really was just young and old. Now David Beckham's 46 and nowhere near his deathbed, we really do need to carve out a new middle. Once we blow demographics and generational differences out of the window, we open up thousands of new ways of looking at each other based on our lifestyles and interests, not age, income or skin colour. We can create a whole new cross-generational landscape.

This cross-generational viewpoint brings a whole new attitude: in the old paradigm we were expected to spend our youth fearing ageing and our old age lamenting the loss of youth. Now there's a whole middle to life and it's fantastic. And something for every woman to look forward to.

It's way too simplistic to believe that the 10, 20, even 30 years we'll live longer than expected are just tacked on to the end of our lives with no added value. These years have been added to the middle, and for midlife women it feels like a new stage in evolution. Many of us are heading toward our sixties with young adults still in our care. Sixty really is the new forty. Yet in our fifties, we are seen as past it but we don't feel it, a recent study showed half of Americans over fifty felt ten years younger than their chronological age and one in six over-sixties felt twenty years younger. Surely it's time for the world to listen to our experience and reset its definitions of age? It makes no sense and a world of talent and experience is being thrown away needlessly. Especially when we have so much to give.

The extraordinary gift of more time.

Most of us have discovered that women really can have everything, just rarely all at once. If we all start demonstrating that the middle is by far the best bit, we can start designing lives with more possibilities than just work, having kids, retiring, death.

# 13

# INSTANTANEOUS

## *The world has changed to meet us*

July 2020

> JANE
>
> You've got to hear the tweet I just saw, hold on ...

Jane scrolls through her Twitter feed.

> JANE
>
> Here we go: 'Errrrr. Out of interest. Does anyone have any idea what's going on? Things feel more uncertain than ever and the tension is palpable. Starting to feel like some marathon with no end and where things get blurry.'

> CAROL
>
> What's so funny about that?

> JANE
>
> His job title is Head of Futures and Insight.

2020 was a strange year. Even for women who've seen so much change in our lives, we've never seen the world change so quickly. At least we were prepared. There really isn't anything that unusual about midlife women staying at home. Many women of our generation choose, or are forced, to have little life outside their own four walls. Who knew you'd all come and join us?

During the first lockdown in March 2020, grown-up kids came home in droves. Family zoom calls replaced nights out with friends. And instead of being the world's greatest embarrassment to our teenage offspring, we actually impressed them with our moves on TikTok. We became important to our children – they were protecting us after all. If one positive thing came out of this whole sorry mess, it was that many of us got to meaningfully connect with those we care the most about.

Of course, others of us were extremely lonely in empty nests, or claustrophobic in housing too small to accommodate everyone all at once. Many endured the 49% rise in domestic violence, and a lot of us were alone by choice or happenstance. For those lucky enough to still have their mums or dads, not being able to see them stole time that can never be reclaimed. And too many of us lost loved ones without the chance to say goodbye.

But there were beautiful things that came out of the lockdown that we should fight to keep. Many of us believe Mother Earth herself stepped in. She stopped the planes and exhaust fumes that were choking her and we increased our daily steps while reducing our carbon footprint. We appreciated all the essential workers who really run the country, gained a greater sense of community and recognised that many of our politicians didn't have the smarts to lead with truth.

As we write this in February 2021, Britain is in a more dreary and joyless third lockdown. Trump is being impeached again – and the Brexit manipulators have left the building. On the bright side, midlife women are poised and ready to take charge. Kamala proves Brown women can do anything, Dr Jill Biden is the first real teacher in the Whitehouse and Stacey Abrams forcefully demonstrated that on-the-ground community action can achieve far more than social media, TV news or the circus rolling into town. There are now vaccines and therapeutics happening, but Covid-19 hasn't just disappeared, like many politicians hoped, and herd immunity was never going to end well for anyone as the daily infection and death rates sadly still demonstrate. The governments who called for us all to prematurely rejoin the rat race now have to face the fact that they can no longer rely on bums on seats in office spaces owned by the banks, billionaires, insurance companies, investment companies and trusts that have been handed down to the landed gentry for centuries to keep the economy running exactly like it always has.

Should the world economy run exactly as it always has?

Is it really going to crash?

While we've been staying home to save lives, the 60% of UK workers who are working from home saved £44.78 per week on commuting and work expenses (a whopping £57.78 in London). That means 23.9 million Brits are saving about £1.1 billion between them every week. And then there's the average five hours per week we no longer spend commuting. Why would we be concerned about the corporations that own the empty spaces when 79% of businesses carried on trading even in the midst of lockdown? Why would they spend fortunes on rent when the business environment needs to change to work around the 88% of workers who want to continue working from home in some capacity? Two-thirds of us have proved we can be just as productive at home as commuting to an office and many are enjoying a better life balance, a closer relationship with their family and recognising just how much time, money and energy they spent to keep a roof over their head when they didn't spend anywhere near enough time under that roof.

Of course, lots of people don't have choices. There will always be jobs that can only be performed out of home and those of us who care for or are vulnerable ourselves are not going to risk anything till there's a proven cure or vaccine, for many an abundance of caution is the only way forward. But even in times of uncertainty there is a way forward, there always is. We're over the shock of an unseen enemy and have altered our lives accordingly. In March 2020, we were pondering what the new normal would be. Now we know the virus isn't going to disappear by magic and it can reappear at any time, we're designing new ways of living, working and socialising. Because we will always live, work and socialise, as humans we will adapt to allow us to find the best way to thrive, we always have we always will.

Companies, organisations and governments have to change faster and work harder than they ever have before. There can be no doubt the economy will take a hit and we will see a redistribution of wealth, some of which will be very unfair. Online businesses and delivery services will see massive profits, bricks and mortar businesses won't fare so well. This is not some political plot, it's capitalism in its purest form – supply and demand.

Most companies expect 22% of their workforce will carry on working remotely full-time and 55% expect workers will work from home one or more days per week. Some tech companies like Twitter and Microsoft have told their employees that they won't ever have to return to the office if they don't want to.

Many people are worried that cities will die. Yet London survived the Black Death, the Great Fire of 1666 and the Blitz – and each time it came back better and stronger. This time, too, we will see new cities; they may house less office space but cities are built around the lives, work and imaginations of their inhabitants. We will find new ways of working using the places where we love to meet. The pension funds, government coffers and businesses of all kinds that rely on bricks and mortar investments will have to diversify their portfolios and create new systems to ensure the economy survives. There will be losses but with careful and creative planning they will be short term and will create better opportunities for the future.

And it's not all doom and gloom. In October 2020, *Fast Company* published an article with the headline, 'We are approaching the fastest, deepest, most consequential technological disruption in history'. It states that humanity is now at a crossroads and that key technologies will converge to completely disrupt the five foundational sectors – information, energy, food, transportation and materials – that underpin our global economy. These developments will undoubtedly benefit society, but they won't be linear. There will be disruptions and there will be major disagreements; those who have the most to lose will fight to keep us locked in the history they have always profited from.

Our government, investment and financial systems are currently built on centuries-old traditions with laws and taxes designed to suit the Agricultural Revolution, rejigged to accommodate the Industrial Revolution and somehow squeezed into the Digital Revolution that will make absolutely no sense in a coming 'Age of Freedom'. They will have to change.

It may be mind-boggling to imagine a world built not on coal, oil, steel, livestock and concrete, but on photons, electrons, DNA, molecules and quantum particles. Where all our food will be grown locally without harmful pesticides, our products will be made predominantly from organic materials and almost everything we use will be designed and developed collaboratively over information networks with the physical production and distribution fulfilled close to home. This could all happen within 10 years at 10% of the cost, using 90% fewer natural resources and 100% less waste. It's not a pipe dream: these advancements are already in development. But for them to prosper ,we have to open our minds to new possibilities and actively push for meaningful societal change to give the world a real chance of eliminating poverty and hunger, halting or even reversing the effects of global warming and creating a work-life balance that's better balanced.

> *'If we hold strong, we can emerge together to create the wealthiest, healthiest, most extraordinary civilization in history. If we do not, we will join the ranks of every other failed civilization for future historians to puzzle over. Our children will either thank us for bringing them an Age of Freedom, or curse us for condemning them to another dark age. The choice is ours.'*
>
> – James Arbib & Tony Seba

We may not believe it, but we're prepared for this too. Midlife women know how to hold strong. We have made it through economic downturns before, many of us have been through all four recessions the world has seen since 1950. Recessions end. But this one will touch every corner of the world and every corner of society; it will be very different. We may face immediate pain; there will certainly be friction with those who cling on to the past and we may feel overwhelmed by some of the losses for us and those around us. But if we can keep looking forward and keep informed and involved, there are solutions to problems we never dreamt we could fix before. What's even better, there's a whole world of new possibilities opening up to everyone – and midlife women have skills and expertise that will be of great value in building a spectacular new normal. Nothing's stopping us, we can't be invisible in a world that isn't here yet, so let's learn and grow and bring good things to the world.

Even if we know little or nothing about tech and what's coming, we can be assured (and we can't say it enough) that new tech will mean our humanity will become our most valuable asset. And midlife women have that in spades. Reports say that 65% of jobs we will do in the future do not currently exist. With AI and machine learning taking over the repetitive and predictable labour tasks employers will prioritise human skills. They call them soft skills. The Collins English dictionary describes them as:

> Desirable qualities for certain forms of employment that do not depend on acquired knowledge: they include common sense, the ability to deal with people, and a positive flexible attitude.

While many tech companies are working out how to measure and grade these skills to fit an algorithm and are running training courses and building apps to teach young adults how to be better humans, we can use our old-fashioned analogue skills to show them how it's done.

Eastern Kentucky University created this top ten list of soft skills most asked for in business executive job listings.

1. Communication
2. Courtesy
3. Flexibility
4. Integrity
5. Interpersonal skills
6. Positive attitude
7. Professionalism

8. Responsibility
9. Teamwork
10. Work ethic

You don't get to the middle of life without mastering almost all of the above. And if you've parented, they're skills you worked hard to pass on to your kids.

So, no matter whether you're going for a job as a barista or barrister, learning skills to start a biotech venture or setting your sights on the board, know you have the immeasurable qualities that modern business and community craves. All you need to do is bring your hard skills up to date and learn new ones to meet these changing times and put yourself out there.

There's never been a better time. And there truly are better times ahead if we all come together and work towards them. Of course, we can't do everything, but we can all do something. We can all speak up. Even if it's just to our closest friends and family. The more we fill the world with our wise words and new ideas the faster the world will change.

We have a duty as the generation with close ties to all living generations to create a new vision for all of them to share too. Because if we think our lives are long, with $700 billion invested in age tech each year, many believe the first generation who will live forever are already here.

We are the shoulders on which they stand.

# 14

# INTERMISSION

## *You're not going mad. It's just menopause.*

Menopause is like pregnancy and a flight to Australia. Long, uncomfortable, and you think it will never end. Then it does. And what's on the other side is so wonderful, you forget all about it the moment it's over.

Like pregnancy, there are a gazillion different things that can happen to your body during menopause and it's a lottery as to which symptoms you will succumb. And each of us experience different symptoms, almost none of which any of us are ever warned about.

Some of the weirder ones include:

- walking into walls
- loss of smell or taste
- wrong words coming out of your mouth
- no words coming out of your mouth
- cold flushes

There are women who swear by (and many who need) HRT to ward off the inevitable loss of fertility. And there are those who decide to face it head-on and get it over with. But no matter how you tackle it, remember this:

*It's just a rewire and reboot. And it ends!*

Yes, for some of us a reboot is just shutting down for a moment then switching ourselves back on and for others it can mean a full network failure but times are changing and, after much campaigning, midlife women are finally getting information about a time in our lives that previously was never spoken about and it's great that women going through biological changes will be given some space to change, but we're also in danger of creating a new stereotype of hot, sweaty, crazy ladies if that's all we see and talk about. We can't allow the image of midlife women to be dominated by a few years of transformation without celebrating the magnificent creatures we transform into.

The internet and your doctor have everything you could ever need to support you through this time (even if you have to push) and a hell of a lot of cool startups are working on keeping us cool, from pyjamas made of thermal materials to bras that monitor emotions. So just look after yourself and look forward. Instead of subconsciously grieving the loss of youth, prepare yourself for the next half of your life.

Take this time when your body is changing to change your mind too. You are becoming a whole new woman with half a life left to live. Use the mood swings to deal with past traumas. Turn your hot flushes into flashes of inspiration. Sweat out all the negativity. And start making new dreams for the future. (With the night sweats, you'll actually be awake enough to write them down!)

Just hang on in there.

The best really is about to come ...

# 15

# INSOUCIANCE

## *The other side of the change*

July 2019

> JANE
>
> I just met a friend at the RHS garden
> in Wisley.

> CAROL
>
> What were you doing there?

> JANE
>
> She's the one who read the first draft
> of the book.

> CAROL
>
> What did she think?

> JANE
>
> She thought I swore too much.

> CAROL
>
> Did you tell her to fuck off?

                    JANE
No, we tried to find a polite version
of 'No fucks left to give'.

                    CAROL
Did you come up with anything?

                    JANE
Insouciance. It means without
care or worry.

                    CAROL
Nah. The original 'French'
works better.

They say you never know what you've got till it's gone, and many of us expected the loss of fertility to be a drag. But after 30 or 40 years of human-making hormones fizzing around your body, you really do appreciate the peace and quiet when they're gone. You wake up every morning feeling exactly the same, a sensation that, bar normal crappy life situations, doesn't change throughout the day, the week or the month. You never burst into tears for no reason or wrack your brain trying to work out why you feel so guilty, or angry, or consume entire tubs of ice cream for any other reason than you want to. And your boobs never hurt. Ever.

What's even better, all that creative energy that used to be reserved for creating human life seems to move from your ovaries straight to your brain, giving you ideas and inspiration like you've never experienced before.

So many women of our age see 'the change' as a chance to change their whole attitude to life, do the things they wished they'd done years ago or start building the life they always wanted. They are going back to school, starting new ventures or taking off on new adventures. In days of old, 'the change' led to the final phase of our lives. These days, it's the gateway to the second half.

> *'At menarche a woman meets her power, during menstruating years she practices her power, at menopause she becomes her power.'*
>
> – Traditional Native American saying

There are downsides, of course: our testosterone levels are proportionally higher which means we'll be plucking hairs from our chin forevermore. Yet that same hormone gives many of us a self-assurance we have never experienced before. It's not just a feeling – research now shows that older women's brains bear a strong resemblance to those of younger men's. Yes, we finally have that level of confidence and it's welcomed; business with men gets easier with less sexual tension in the room and what had once been perceived as overconfidence rather beautifully turns into gravitas, hysteria becomes passion and things that were hard to fight for become hard-earned experience.

It's time to be seen and heard. Because we really don't give a flying fuck what anyone thinks anymore. This doesn't mean we don't care what people think – we just don't care what *everyone* thinks about us. It's not possible to spend this long on earth without realising there are some people that we really can't stand or agree with, which means there are plenty of folks who'll feel the same way about us. Many of us have spent way too long people-pleasing, saying 'yes' when we mean 'no' (and vice-versa) and keeping quiet when we really should have spoken up. We really don't have the time or patience for that anymore.

Once you have got over the loss of being able to make humans, you start to appreciate the gifts of being your own woman. It comes as no surprise that the majority of cosmetic procedures are carried out on women in their forties who can't imagine life without being judged on their looks alone. But this world does exist. And it is very comfortable.

When we no longer face a societal pressure to be pleasing to the eye, we no longer have to grin and bear high heels, tight jeans or bras unless we choose to. We can get away with just a simple skincare regime and instead of painting our faces, we can choose to paint pictures or walls or a new future. There is great freedom in focusing less on how the world sees us to looking for what we can bring to the world. The first half of our lives have been all about us and what we can build; the second is more about everyone and what we are going to leave behind.

It's time to shout about our new-found power. Our super-honesty.

> *'One day an army of gray-haired old ladies may very quietly take over the world.'*
>
> – Gloria Steinem

Of course, some of us still bite our lips, especially when we have the wisdom to know when not to waste our words, but a hell of a lot of midlife women need to tell the world what they think in no uncertain terms. Especially in times when truth seems so hard to find and people are afraid of what they'll lose if they point out what's wrong. When we have zero fucks left to give, our brutal honesty is the thing the world so desperately needs right now.

As we write, 60% of all employees in the UK now work from home – yet 70% of childrearing and household chores are still done by women. With the additional burden of home-schooling, many report their domestic workload has jumped from 75% to 90%. Women are frazzled and our economic equality has been pushed back. We now won't reach parity in our lifetime. It's a gift we'll pass on to our great-granddaughters. Sorry.

The figures that are coming out about job losses due to Covid-19 are terrifying. As the business world recalibrates there will be job losses and all the early data shows that Covid is going to have the biggest economic impact on women, whose jobs are 1.8 times more vulnerable to this crisis than men's. Women make up 39% of global employment, but account for 54% of overall job losses.

The latest reports say women are being forced back to where we were in the 1950s.

We say, NOT. ON. OUR. WATCH.

In the UK, paid maternity leave for all women only arrived 21 years ago, and childcare was rare so a hell of a lot of us were forced out of or had to scale back our careers for exactly these reasons. It's time to pioneer again.

We are the first generation of women to go through menopause in the workforce en masse and we need to challenge the patriarchal career structure based on a man's physiology, where 35 is seen as the career sweet spot – when they are in their prime. This is sheer cruelty to women who face the reality of their biological clock set to explode as the career doomsday clock set to 35 looms. Now so many women struggle balancing careers with young children and interrupted childcare, midlife women need to step up to the plate. If the workplace needs to be manned by those not hamstrung by kids, we need to pioneer women's careers again. If the coronavirus brings a return to testosterone-packed workplaces, we've got to have the balls to get back in and do what we did the first time – pave the way for all the women behind us.

We need to create a new generation of female leaders

because for the first time in the history of man there are finally enough women who have reached a woman's prime – midlife. We can forge a new leadership structure, one that is tried and tested in the natural world. We're the only land-based animals that don't breed to death. When orcas and pilot whales go through menopause, they become the leaders of their pods. Who better to have every whale's best interests at heart than the cow that gave birth to them all? We should become more like orcas and pilot whales. We need leaders who care about all of us.

*'I've been your age. You've never been mine.'*

– Mrs E. Evans, Jane's grandma

A longer career line for women with leadership gained when wisdom is acquired will mean earth mothers won't disappear from business and modern businesswomen don't have to become more like men to succeed.

When women who have made choices, both good and bad, who have surrounded themselves with people whose life experience they've learnt from, start making decisions, we will design work practices that have everyone's best interests at heart.

On the current career timeline only a few women have the alchemic formula that even allows them the time and space to dedicate to a career. They don't have children either by choice or fate and enjoy a life where their career can be a major focus. They have the income to sustain solid support structures that allow them to have a family and a major career focus. They have a partner who will raise the children. They have a mother, friend, sister or auntie who'll raise their kids too. They earn so little they get free or subsidised childcare.

On the surface, it would seem that childcare is the number one priority and has certainly been the focus of equality efforts to date. But feminism to us was always about choice, and we seem to have lost a choice that only a longer career path can offer.

One in five women are still concerned about going back to work after maternity leave. We're still expected to hide our vulnerability and act like men. And some women just don't have the courage to fight instincts that have been there since the beginning of time. Others see their kids as their greatest creation and nothing could ever be more important – especially not a job. And some have children whose needs make it impossible to go back to a career, no matter how meticulously planned.

Regardless of our circumstances or which sort of mothers we are, one thing's for sure, once we're responsible for growing human beings, we will NEVER have 100% brain space for our careers.

*'Everyone talks about side hustle these days. I'm a single mum to three teenagers. That's my side hustle. What do they want me to do? Start a micro-brewery? Knit vaginas?'*

– Sue Higgs

So it's no surprise that young women fret over their fertility. They're vulnerable and making major life decisions out of fear. Or leaving their babies, when every ounce of their biology is screaming at them not to.

Of course, some women are superwomen and can do it all with ease. But we unfairly pile expectations on ourselves when we expect all women to put on a brave face, especially at times when we are physically, emotionally and financially vulnerable.

Most midlife women have tried to be superwomen and few have prevailed. But now may be the time to prove we can have it all – just not all at once.

Midlife women have everything that modern business is looking for. But the societal narrative throws a cloak of invisibility over the magic, profit and success we could bring.

One of the hardest things about running the Uninvisibility Project is hearing the stories of brilliant women fighting just to keep a roof over their heads: the ex-television director who wipes the bum of an elderly rich man with Alzheimer's; the once great TV presenter applying for a job as a hotel maid, or the PR whizz driving a bus. Then add the stories of redundancy on hitting 45 and the nightmares of job hunting with too much experience. It's heartbreaking and demoralising. Especially when the only jobs that welcome us with open arms are minimum-wage care roles. Particularly nannies. Seriously, just because we raised kids doesn't make us naturals. And it certainly doesn't warrant being our only available career choice.

This presumption isn't just societal. It's much closer to home than that. Many women of our generation are emotionally blackmailed into free childcare by our children. Which begs the question; has the job market/algorithm become so specialised and 'of the minute' that we have sentenced the generation who fought against domestic servitude into a life of housekeeping because that's the last role we played?

When did we become so undervalued? And it's not just at the top end of town.

One story we heard was of a 65-year-old nurse who was encouraged to take retirement and then come back as a volunteer. It was very noble of her and we all should do our bit to help the NHS, but the state pension is only a fraction of a regular salary. This is the patriarchy taking advantage of our natural carers' good natures.

It's probably time for even the nicest of us to get a little nasty.

The first women in history with genuine employment experience in almost all fields of endeavour have been relegated to minimum-wage handmaids and unpaid servants.

We have to stand up and we have to fight.

Starting with tough love.

Tell your daughter/-in-law to look after her own damn kids. Then actually show her how to pick up her career and run with it when she's finished. Almost universally, grandparents report that they love their grandkids as much as they did their own, but the best bit, by far, is handing them back. How cruel is it that societal pressure puts an expectation on women who have been through all the hard yards of adult-rearing to repeat it all over again every Monday to Friday? Of course, many of us are in the perfect position to help out and love to. But it has to be a choice. And not one that costs your future financial security and theirs.

We don't want our kids to have to pay for a nation of older women living in poverty. It's already happening in Australia, where 50% of all women over 70 and 34% of single women over 50 are already below the breadline. We don't want to leave a planet where women earn less than men. And we certainly don't want to leave the planet in the mess it's in right now.

Whatever path we chose in life there can be no doubt we need more female leaders. Grown women in the ad industry have fan-girled Cindy Gallop for years. For her, midlife was not a period of invisibility, it was a catalyst for change.

### Cindy Gallop

**Cindy Gallop was headed for Oxford University the moment she popped out of the womb – whether she liked it or not. Her English**

grandfather died when her father was just 17. He dropped out, travelled the world – motorbiked across America, worked in a travelling carnival in Australia – and fetched up in Singapore where he met Cindy's Chinese mother. They ended up back in England with young daughters, but her father didn't have a university degree, a fact he regretted. He took a variety of low-paying jobs while studying for a degree late in life. Cindy's childhood, characterised by excessive academic pressure with no choice, made her slightly resentful.

Until the moment she stepped onto the hallowed ground of Somerville College Oxford and realised what privilege her tiger mother 'par excellence' and ambitious father had relentlessly pushed her towards and the extra work and pressure to secure a scholarship had been worth it. She took to Oxford like a duck to water. Especially Oxford's vibrant student drama scene – she wrote, acted, directed and stage-managed student productions, while dreaming of a life in the theatre.

Now, Cindy is one of those women who knows how to make her dreams come true. She soon had a career in theatre marketing, but it didn't pay anywhere near enough to match all her expectations, so she found her way into the glamorous world of advertising and diligently made her way to the top. Then stopped. 'I always thought one's 45th birthday is the moment when you should pause, take stock, reflect and review, where have I been, where am I going?'

Vast amounts of thought and angst ensued.

Eventually Cindy decided if she wanted to review every possible option open for what was effectively the second half of her life, maybe the best thing to do was to put herself on the market very publicly and say, *'Okay, guys, here I am. What have you got?'* And see what comes. She took a massive leap into the unknown and resigned as chairman of BBH New York without a job to go to. It was the best bloody thing she ever did. She became an immediate convert to working for oneself.

'You know, the thing is, too many people think that a job is the safe option,' she said. 'It's not. In a job, you're at the complete mercy of management changes, industry downturns, marketplace dynamics. I always say to people, whose hands would you rather place your future in? Those of a large corporate entity that doesn't give a shit about you, or somebody who'll always have your best interests at heart – i.e. you.'

Of course, Cindy's destiny found her. She had just started consulting when an old client asked her to partner with him on a new social media platform. She quickly discovered when working with developers how creative tech was and started to project her own ideas with absolutely no idea what was technically possible. Her project manager on her first startup IfWeRanTheWorld put it very simply: 'If you can write it down, we can build it.'

Since then Cindy's gone on to build MakeLoveNotPorn, a user-generated, human-curated social sex video-sharing platform. It started with her discovery 13 years ago through her personal experience dating younger men, that when we don't talk openly and honestly about sex, porn becomes sex education by default. Cindy originally launched MLNP as a 'Porn World vs Real World' little side venture. The extraordinary global response to her 2009 TED talk about it made her realise she'd uncovered a huge global social issue, and she turned it into a business. Cindy decided to apply social media dynamics to the one area no social network or platform will touch, to socialise and normalise sex in the real world in order to promote consent, communication, good sexual values and good sexual behaviour.

She also built it to make 'an absolute goddamn fucking shit ton of money', something she encourages us all to do: 'You can then fund other women, support other women, donate to other women, help other women. We need to build our own financial ecosystem, because the white male one isn't working for us.'

### How to add 'Cindy Power' to your life and business

#### BE A CHAMPION.

Cindy does not buy into the myth of female competition. Throughout her entire career, she has never experienced another woman being bitchy to her; she has always worked in an environment of collaboration and representation. She represents.

Even though she left the advertising industry,

she holds one of its most important roles: she speaks up. Well before #MeToo, Cindy was alerting the industry to the lack of female representation and the key role sexual harassment plays in managing women out of every industry. She stood up and shouted about how few people of colour were in every company. She challenged ageism and the failure to value older people – or 'experts' as she likes to call us. She asks questions others can't.

Ask questions.

## GET TO A POINT WHERE IT DOESN'T MATTER WHAT OTHER PEOPLE THINK.

One of the reasons Cindy can be a mouthpiece for people is she is not beholden to the massive global concerns that run the industry. Many humans are silenced because they work, do business or want to sell their business to a massive holding company one day. Cindy starts essential conversations but she does not see herself as brave: she thinks the most junior person in the room, who voices their opinion, or the only voice in a boardroom who questions the make-up of the people sitting around the table, are brave – she actively works to embolden others to make change.

Keep the conversations going.

## TECH IS YOUR WAY OUT.

Cindy doesn't believe her industry will change fast enough (if at all) and advises any woman frustrated by the lack of progress to take her experience and digitise it. Investors love 'adtech' so there's money to be made when women – the primary target of a ludicrously male-dominated ad industry – build our own adtech ventures to sell to ourselves. Women can do this in any industry, because we don't have to be a tech person to have ideas that drive change – we can hire tech people to build it, just as Cindy did. So, let's make something filled with our massive experience that solves a problem or opens up a new opportunity and then we're on our way to building the sort of companies and products that will thrive.

What could you build that would make your industry better?

### DON'T BE AFRAID TO SELL OUT – PLAN FOR IT!

For some reason, there is a belief that women are supposed to build small businesses that eventually fade away. Men openly start businesses with the sole aim of being bought out by a larger concern. The irony is, the ones that are most successful are usually built on an opinion or viewpoint that would have been gagged by a holding company. Breaking away to solve an unseen problem or take advantage of a revenue stream the big boys can't reach is, in many ways, the only way to bring innovation into industries that are set in their ways. So, the question is what could you build for your industry that it would want to buy back?

Of course, we can't all be champions of industry, but we can be champions of each other. We need to muster all the insouciance we have. Just because we have zero fucks left to give, it does not mean we don't give a fuck, especially when there's so much fuckery going on.

We've just got to get on with it because we may be living longer lives, but life is still way too short.

# 16

# INCURABLE

*We're not getting any younger*

October 2020

> JANE
> How are you feeling?

> CAROL
> Oh you know, another night of three
> sheets and two duvets. How's the thumb?

> JANE
> Writing's really painful when it
> hurts too. I tell you, trackpads aren't
> designed for us with less-evolved
> opposable thumbs. I've bandaged it up
> and am battling on.

> CAROL
> Aren't you worried?

> JANE
> I was, then I saw this old bloke with
> a pair of brain-controlled robotic

```
gloves playing the piano for the first
time in 20 years. If it packs up com-
pletely I'm getting me some of those.
```

We would be lying if we said that everything's rosy about growing older. It has its drawbacks, most of them physical. You can't inhabit a body for over 45 years without wear and tear – a lot of it can be fixed or hidden but there's no cure for ageing: none of us are getting out of here alive.

Or with 25-year-old skin. If beauty is skin deep, then we have to dig deep to ensure we don't fall into the trap of believing that we should hold onto youthful looks at all costs. When we write a new narrative for midlife women it has to be one of choice, especially on how we look.

Why would we judge Angela Merkel on her complexion instead of her leadership and innate understanding of science? Who cares if Nancy Pelosi's had 'work' done, when she does such a good job? Would Tracey Ullman be as funny if she struggled to raise an eyebrow?

Of course, we can choose to enhance our appearance, but it shouldn't be expected of us.

One in three American women are considering getting work done, 26% of whom said it was down to 'wanting to appear youthful at work' or 'looking for or starting a new job'. Add that to the fact that a third of the long-term unemployed are over 50 and we can understand why any woman would be afraid of looking her age.

*'If I wanted to be prettier, fillers, Botox and a neck lift might help – but I think I'm past all that. My feelings come out in my face and show who I am inside in ways that words can't express.'*

– Diane Keaton

The advances in cosmetic surgery are astounding. And all good feminists agree that choice and equity are at the heart of everything we stand for. That includes the choice of how we look.

Some choose the power of smooth skin over the power of micro-expressions. Some of us hide our wrinkles; some believe we've earned them. Lauren Bacall famously said, 'your whole life shows in your face and you should be proud of that.'

One thing's for sure, midlife women are not going to become completely visible till we stop hiding our age and see women who are proud of their time-marked beauty too. Even the supermodels are fighting for it. As Paulina Porizkova said:

> The thing I'm really battling with is that I think we should all have the right, or at least the ability, to be beautiful for who we are, and not for being surgically altered. If you want to be, that's totally cool and there's nothing wrong with it, but we're doing away with reality to an extent, and that really bothers me because now you're not supposed to be old.

When we stop deceiving ourselves that youth is better, we will stop the beauty industry from deceiving us about their products. There isn't an anti-ageing cream on this planet that works.

Dame Anita Roddick told us this 20 years ago: 'Moisturisers do work, but the rest is complete pap. There is nothing on God's planet, not one thing, that will take away 30 years of arguing with your husband and 40 years of environmental abuse. Anything which says it can magically take away your wrinkles is a scandalous lie. You would be better off spending the money on a good bottle of pinot noir.'

The first 10 to 14 layers of our skin are dead. Gone. Deceased. Pushing up daisies. Meeting their maker. And a cream made of water, powder and maybe some light-reflecting particles isn't going to bring those skin cells back. Even if they contain stem cells from discarded baby foreskins.

The hyper-expensive ones contain ingredients that tighten and puff up our skin. Any effects they have are temporary – some only last for a few minutes, which is all they need to trick us into believing they work.

Of course, there's nothing wrong with spending money to look good, but the rich women who take great pleasure in or make a living from how they look, know the only way to achieve it is with lasers burning off their skin, paralysing their facial muscles, or undergoing the knife. And even when women do all that, they rarely look younger. Just altered.

Black women crack up about all this.

They've been slathering themselves in shea butter, paw paw cream or homebrand moisturiser since birth. And they rarely tell you their age. You probably wouldn't believe them anyway. White women have to stop believing the bullshit!

### Vikki Ross

**Vikki Ross started her copywriting career at Dame Anita Roddick's The Body Shop. Anita would never tell a woman to believe or achieve unrealistic goals set by the beauty industry. And she'd never sell a product on false promises. As such, Vikki learnt the tricks the rest of the trade relied upon – and avoided them. Here, she lets us in on some insider secrets.**

*Maybe it's ... made up.*

Ah the beauty of the beauty industry. A world of lotions and potions that promise everything but do nothing. Nothing in a cream or cleanser can remove lines, smooth wrinkles, or turn back time. But the ads, websites and products claim they do. Don't they?

### It's all in the application.

A space here. A full-stop or question mark there. And a load of meaningless words. They're the tricks of the trade – the tricks a beauty brand uses to get past lawyers and advertising regulations. And you.

In an ad for Clinique's Even Better Skin Tone Corrector, the headline invites you to imagine the product benefit:

*Imagine erasing past damage to create a more even tone*

But it doesn't promise it, because it can't claim it. If it could, the headline would straight up say:

*Erase past damage to create a more even tone*

Why can't Clinique claim their product erases past damage to create a more even tone? Well, what exactly is past damage? We know what they're implying – they're implying the effects of ageing. They can't say that because they can't claim that, because nothing in a lotion or potion can erase how anyone's skin has changed and evolved over time. And nothing can change the skin's texture to even it out either.

On their website, Clinique also promotes their Smart Clinical MD range. The headline asks:

*Not ready for needles?*

Clinique absolutely can't claim that their products act as an alternative to needles – Botox – so they imply it. And they wrap it up in a question that they don't answer, relying on the reader to make the connection: their products are as effective as Botox so they'll remove wrinkles. Even the range name is designed to imply an impressive combination of innovation (smart) and medical or surgical procedures (clinical).

*If you really didn't ever want to get wrinkles, then you should have stopped smiling years ago!*

Dame Anita Roddick

### Here comes the science bit.

Creams and cleansers are a mix of powder and water. There's nothing in them that can do anything more than cleanse and moisturise skin. Anti-ageing creams contain pearl pigments or iridescent particles – tiny shiny things that reflect light so skin looks bright. Until it's cleansed and toned and any faux glow is washed and wiped away.

Here's what Olay claims its Illuminating eye cream can do:

*Instantly brightens eyes by reducing the look of dark circles*

That'll be those light reflectors. They're like glitter, glistening on the skin so it appears radiant but isn't really. So you see, that last bit – the look of dark circles – isn't promising anything. It means dark circles appear to be less dark, but they aren't.

A cream can't change skin colour. Unless it's tinted. And if it's tinted then it's make-up, not skincare. Want to get rid of dark circles? Sleep more.

### Beyond the pale.

While some people are busy brightening their skin, others are lightening theirs. Or so they think. Paris offers a whole range of whitening products. It's called White Perfect, which raises the racist alarm. But do whiteners whiten?

L'Oréal Paris says online: 'Our skin whitening products work to fade dark spots and brighten skin to give you the fair, flawless complexion you desire.'

They say they 'work to' deliver on their products' promises but they don't say they do work. It's like they're working at it, rather than they worked it out. But their White Perfect Whitening & Moisturizing Toner is so bold by name, it must work. Right? It's a toner – a clear liquid. It couldn't possibly do anything more than feel refreshing.

Save some cash and splash water on your face instead.

### Beauty from within.

If we believe everything beauty brands tell us – and buy everything beauty brands sell us – we

**fill our face with useless products, and our minds with empty promises.**

**Artificial beauty is only skin deep. Real beauty is within. It's invisible under the weight of made-up marketing. Let it out. Make it visible.**

Now you know the tricks of the trade, read this 2019 copy for La Mer moisturiser from their website, and see if it actually says it will make any difference or even makes the slightest scrap of sense:

> This luxuriously rich cream deeply soothes, moisturizes and helps heal away dryness. Skin looks naturally vibrant, restored to its healthiest center. Miracle Broth™ – the legendary healing elixir that flows through all of La Mer – infuses skin with sea-sourced renewing energies. Ideal for drier skin.

This 'miracle potion' costs about £350 for a 100 ml jar.

If ever there was a time in our lives to stop buying myths, it's now. If you're reading this and have a bottle in your bathroom, when it's empty, pop down to Boots for a replacement, then donate the money you save to a theatre that desperately needs your patronage or invest in a friend's startup.

Let's all start buying shea butter or paw paw cream, home-brand moisturiser or a pot of something special from the woman down the road. If we'd done that at 30 and put what we saved on even the most basic of anti-ageing creams into our pensions we'd have been £65,000 richer at 70.

We've got to get smarter about stuff like this. And we have to demand the next generations of women aren't fooled out of their wealth too. We're not trying to destroy the cosmetic industry. We'll always love beauty products. And we'll always love spoiling ourselves. We love skin creams – how they feel, how they smell and how they make our skin feel and we'll buy them in line with what we can afford. But we can't afford to be conned out of a happy second half of life. Anti-ageing is offensive to women coming into their power.

We need to demand realistic products. And change the narrative.

When we see more than just the unattainable images of beautiful older women, with good genes and good plastic surgeons, we'll create a new standard of beauty. One that everyone can achieve.

Let's rejoice in the beauty of our lives not our faces.

And let's not forget the woman who changed our views on beauty:

### Dame Anita Roddick

Anyone who saved up their pocket money for a Body Shop strawberry face wash or treated themself to a pineapple scrub in the 1980s and 1990s, do NOT google the woman who brought a little joy and excitement (in a little recyclable bottle) to our lives. Much of Dame Anita Roddick's history has been written by people who didn't understand her vision. Even one of her obituaries threw extraordinary shade.

From the outset Anita Roddick was a myth-maker. One of the most lauded and yet controversial     businesswomen     of     her

generation, she specialised in apparently breaking the rules. She was a pioneering woman in a man's world. She turned a cottage industry selling hand-made products into a global brand worth millions. She lambasted the 'pin-striped dinosaurs' of the City, despite the fact that they were financing her. She embraced green issues before they were fashionable. She averred that shopping was a moral choice. And she insisted that making money and making the world a better place were not incompatible. That was her triumph. Her tragedy was that in the end she came to believe her own PR.
– *Independent*, September 2007

Her tragedy was she didn't have time to finish the job. She never got to live in an era where her ideas would be seen as common sense, not crackpot fantasies. Anita was cruelly taken from us in 2007 by complications from hepatitis C which she contracted from a contaminated blood transfusion. She was just 64 years old.

Did Anita fail? The pin-striped dinosaurs certainly believed she did. They painted her as a hypocrite for selling out – to them. But what did she do with their money? She built three orphanages in Romania, an organic farm cooperative in Nicaragua, numerous health and education projects in India, a brazil nut cooperative in Brazil, a healthcare initiative in Nepal, a shea and cocoa butter cooperative in Ghana, a soap-making factory in Scotland – and that was just where her money went while she was alive.

Anita walked the walk as well as she talked
the talk. She didn't regret 'selling out': she did it
for the right reasons. She started her little shop
in Brighton in 1976, not to make a fortune but to
survive. Her husband had gone on a romantic
adventure to ride a horse from Buenos Aires to
New York and she needed to provide for their
two young daughters. With her simple idea and
brilliant storytelling skills, one shop quickly
became two. In 1978, her husband unsaddled
and returned to find Anita had built a thriving
business. They devised a franchise model that
would allow other women to join the business
and share in their good fortune. They floated
on the stock exchange to cope with a business
growing quicker than they could handle, and by
1991 there were 700 Body Shop stores around
the country.

To Anita though, they weren't just shops:
they were 700 massive billboards in high-traffic
areas to promote what she was really selling.
Ecology. Fair Trade. Real beauty. Positive body
image. Community. Ethical business. Animal
rights. Human rights. And a call to save the
goddamned planet! All concepts that had been
swept under the rug in the 'greed is good' 1980s'.
The yuppies hated having a hippy in their midst
and it was decidedly mutual. Anita detested the
fact a Haitian worker making clothes for Disney
would have to work for 166 years to earn what
Michael Eisner (the head of Disney at the time)
earned in a day. He wasn't even the world's seventh richest man: if those who were pooled their
wealth, they could eliminate global poverty

immediately. They never raised a finger. She raised hell!

As she wrote in *Business as Usual* (2000), 'Nomadic capital never sets down roots, never builds communities. It leaves behind toxic wastes, embittered workers and indigenous communities driven out of existence.'

Brilliant, inspirational and beautifully flawed, Anita's only real mistake was losing the reins of her heart-led business. Few could believe she would sell out to the enemy – big cosmetics. But in 2006, L'Oréal purchased the Body Shop's 3,000 stores in 65 countries for a whopping £652 million. She took the money and ran toward her real goal. On her death, she dedicated her whole fortune (over £50m) to global charities which continue her work to this very day.

Anyone who followed her story in real time wishes she was still here. She's exactly the sort of strong, empathetic leader the world could do with right now.

We can take heart that Anita is having the last laugh. Her loving husband, Gordon, started a political activism platform in her memory. Its very name sounds exactly like the sort of powerful brand she would conceive (and giggle about): 38 Degrees takes its name from the angle at which snowflakes come together to form an avalanche. Now two million members in Britain can start petitions for community issues to ensure the powerful are held to account and stand for a fairer world. Every petition signed carries a little bit of Anita's spirit.

*Get angry. But get angry for the right reasons.*
*And fucking do something with the anger. There's*
*power in that.*

### How can we carry on Anita's work?

'IF YOU PUT HUMANITY FIRST, GOOD BUSINESS
WILL FOLLOW.'

Anita's beauty business was not an original idea,
women all over the world have been concocting
and selling potions for us to feel more beautiful
for millennia. Her secret ingredient was hope
for a better world. When you used one of her
ethically sourced products you felt like you were
saving the whales, enriching remote communities or sticking a finger up to corporate greed.
Anita's business was not built around little
bottles of sweet-smelling potions. It was built
around her well-defined personal philosophy.
Every business decision was made in line with
her truth. Know your truth.

'NEVER UNDERESTIMATE THE POWER OF STO-
RIES – OF CREATIVITY – TO DRIVE CHANGE AND
TO OPEN HEARTS. PEOPLE DON'T JUST SEE PAS-
SION. THEY FEEL IT. AND IT MATTERS.'

Everything is built on a story. And every story
is a PR opportunity. The first Body Shop started
in a small shop in Brighton squeezed between
two funeral parlours. When the neighbours
complained her trading name was distasteful,
Anita took the story straight to the local paper.

Soon people were flocking to see what all the fuss was about. They found a quaint little shop with weird little bottles and handwritten labels (little did anyone know they were actually urine sample bottles – the only ones she could afford). Each told the story of the product, where it was from, its history, you could add the fragrance of your choice and bring your precious little bottle back to be refilled. You became part of the story. When you entered the Body Shop, you entered the whole world of beauty and learnt ancient secrets of women in distant lands. So much more powerful than the cosmetic industry's stories of unattainable beauty in a perfect world few could aspire to. Find your story. Tell your truth.

'I LOVE TACTICS; I DON'T LIKE PLANS.'

Dame Anita was against animal testing because she couldn't comprehend how anyone could do such a thing. She never planned to change British law; her tactic was to start the conversation. She then added another tactic and another ...

As Michelle Thew, chief executive of the British Union for the Abolition of Vivisection, said, Roddick was pivotal to them. 'When we started, testing of cosmetic ingredients and products on animals in the UK was universal, and the cosmetic companies said you couldn't do it any other way, Anita showed that you could. She and the Body Shop provided a model to show the companies you could do it differently, and most importantly, they offered shoppers in the high street a choice. And she was inspiring, with campaigning and petitions. She was absolutely pivotal.'

It took 11 years of consistent campaigning not planning to get the Animals (Scientific Procedures) Act through parliament. Stick with tactics, change tactics, use shock tactics and you can plan on succeeding.

'IT'S A CRAZY, COMPLICATED JOURNEY. IT REALLY IS EXPERIMENT, EXPERIMENT, EXPERIMENT.'

Even after 20 successful years in business, Anita viewed the Body Shop as an experiment. She was always tinkering. Failures turned into new opportunities. U-turns provided a different view. Speed, agility and responsiveness, she believed, was the key to all future success. Good ideas can always be improved on. Keep improving your ideas.

'I CAN'T PRETEND THAT OUR TRADING PRACTICES OFFER A SOLUTION TO EVERYBODY'S NEEDS.'

When Anita started her business there was no such thing as 'fair trade'. Once again, she was making it up as she went along. The pin-stripe dinosaurs wanted her to make money for them; she wanted women all over the world to make lasting profit for their families and communities. Anita preferred to be measured by how she treated the weaker and frailer communities she traded with, rather than the size of her profits. No wonder she made enemies. You can't be all things to all people. You can't please all the people all the time. All you can do is your best.

'MAKE THE PAST INTO THE PROLOGUE FOR THE FUTURE.'

Almost every word Anita spoke then could come out of the mouth of one of today's progressive leaders. Her book, *Business as Unusual*, was one of the first moves toward greater corporate responsibility and accountability. Now brands have purpose and whole startup ecosystems are dedicated to creating the sort of planet-saving businesses Anita dreamed of.

We should listen to the most important advice she left for us.

'I don't believe the most visible changes in companies of the future will be in the so-called 'science' of business, but in who works for you, why they're doing it and what their work means to them ...'

# 17

# INFILTRATE

*Let's get to work*

March 2016

> CAROL
> How's the job-hunting going?

> JANE
> Terrible. I'm pretty sure there's some-
> thing wrong with the algorithm for
> women of our age. I got an email this
> morning from a recruitment agency
> saying they'd found the perfect job for
> me. A secretarial assistant!

> CAROL
> You what?

> JANE
> I know. How's it going with the script?

> CAROL
> They want me to give the Black barris-
> ter a white girlfriend.

In August 2020, the Centre for Better Ageing and the Learning and Work Institute released alarming figures that older workers on unemployment benefits had doubled during the pandemic. There can be no doubt that midlife women face an employment crisis. This is nothing new to us.

We were the generation of the 1-in-10. Everyone knew what a UB40 was – the employment benefit form from the Job Centre. In the seventies and eighties, 10% unemployment was treated as a national crisis.

Before Covid-19, we were the 1-in-3 generation. A third of unemployed midlife women faced long-term unemployment. In other words, it doesn't look like we'll ever work again.

This ageism hits both men and women. But it hits women harder. We only have a third of men's retirement savings and 1.2 million of us in Britain have no private pension savings at all.

Now it's even worse, many of us need to stay at home because we or someone we love is vulnerable, and our kids who relied on retail and hospitality jobs have joined us in the unemployable pile, so it looks like a lot of us will be feeding grown-up kids with our non-existent paycheques for a while to come.

We have to get back to work. And we have to start saving now.

Because this gift of extra life comes at a price. The dream of retiring and sailing off into the sunset at 55 has passed for all but a few alphas who made the world believe they were smarter than everyone else. But in the long game, we have the skills to build empires that will enrich us all.

*'We have to be visible. We shouldn't be ashamed of who we are. We have to show the world that we are numerous. There are many of us out there.'*

– Sylvia Rivera

We're now seeing the first women in business who have a lived experience of the challenges of being working women, working mothers, businesswomen during menopause and the long-term effects of the gender pay gap. Many are still the only women of their age in the business. Those women were never in competition with other women, they were playing a long game for all of us.

And it was a numbers game.

The old trope is that one woman on a board turned into one of the boys, two allowed them to have a voice and three allowed them to make change. Don't believe the myth: those first women never became one of the boys. They were just biding their time till they could put new ideas into practice, such as 'amplification', with one famous example coming from Barack Obama's presidency. When Obama took office in 2008, two-thirds of his top aides were men. Women found they had to elbow their way into important meetings and, even once inside, they would struggle to be heard. The women adopted a strategy of amplification. When a woman came up with an idea another woman would repeat it, giving credit to her. This forced the men to recognise her contribution and stopped them claiming her ideas as their own. It worked: when Obama started his second term, half of his top aides were women.

Shine theory is another positive mantra we can all practise in every area of our lives and all our relationships. It was first conceived by Anne Friedman and businesswoman Amanita Sow to describe a concerted effort to collaborate with, rather than compete against, other people – in particular, other women. Shine theory shows that true confidence is infectious. Put simply, 'If you don't shine – I don't shine'.

It's time for us all to amplify each other and shine together. Now we have women who have completed the career timeline, let's rip it up and start again. The current kill or be killed career trajectory is designed to suit a man's biology and temperament, starting in their physical prime at entry level where they jostle for the best positions and continuing with the fight to become top dog before their hairline recedes completely to get the key to the lift to the penthouse suite, where they'll live in luxury until they retire on a pot of gold or a handshake.

All fight or flight and not enough tend and befriend.

This has to change.

Clever women can get ahead of the curve. But it's going to take a lot of hard work, research and soul searching to find the right path forward. There has never been a more important time for the amazing women of business, government, charity and the PTA to take the lead in a new direction.

Women who have carried us all on their shoulders still need to go that extra mile. They need to show the legions of women behind them just what they can do when they are at their most powerful, and demonstrate just how successful long careers can be. But it's not only at the very top. The world needs more wise women. And wise women need work.

Especially the women who chose career paths or had life paths that made their career their major focus. To throw away all that experience when they are hitting the most powerful point in their lives is just stupidity. This is the time to promote them. We may be a bit more expensive than a younger person, but we're faster, make fewer mistakes and don't waste time trying things we've tried before. We can also build new diverse, female-friendly work environments that find ways of employing more women who are coming back from putting family first, no matter how long they've been gone.

We'll find creative ways to encourage them to return. If one in five young women is apprehensive about returning to the workforce after having a baby, imagine the abject terror of someone who's been absent for 20 years? The level of bravery required to enter a career for the first time in the second half of life is true valour.

The best place to start is where you left off. It's rare for our generation to have given up work completely, most of us simply scaled down. Look for ways you can build on your experience and learn new skills. Spend time researching recent reports and articles about your field of work, particularly where it is projected to go in the future.

Don't be afraid of tech. You're probably reading this book on it. It's part of life, and you have the basic skills. And there are plenty of ways of learning new ones. Smash ageism and apply for every learning opportunity going, even if all the pictures they show are 18-year-olds. Do your research; there are courses to fit every budget. Or you could just do what the kids do and YouTube it. There are free tutorials on practically everything.

Don't worry if you're not technical. There are plenty of people on this planet who can code and build. What most industries need is the humans to come up with the ideas to code. And certainly, don't be concerned that you've never done it before, especially when so many jobs we could do haven't even been invented yet. The advances in AI and robotics are not going to diminish the workforce, they're just going to change it.

Be ready.

Starting again doesn't have to take a truckload of bravery and self-confidence. Most of it comes from hard work, study and following what truly interests you.

### Bushra Burge

**Bushra Burge is a phenomenal woman. She graduated from Imperial College, London, with a degree in Biochemistry and Management, but**

the first job she got straight out of university was working on databases for the Y2K scare in finance, investment banks and insurance companies because, after being a poor student, it was a job where she could earn money, maybe even accrue some savings and, you know, eat.

Working in the creative industries was the furthest thing from her mind, because she didn't know anyone in the creative sector. She hadn't met or spoken to anyone working anywhere outside of finance, tech or restaurants. She didn't know if there was a place for someone like her. What she did know though was that new things excited her, that her curiosity was piqued by innovation. So, during her stint coding databases, Bushra started to explore her options and began taking part-time courses in creative subjects. She did magic, art and various fashion courses, the latter at the London College of Fashion. In the early days, she was shy. Her design illustrations were small. So small her tutor had to blow them up so he could see them. He'd chuckle as he asked why they were so small, and she'd shrug. He'd tell her they were good. At first, she thought he was just being nice.

Then one day, as Bushra was taking yet another of his classes, the tutor suggested she take a part-time fashion degree. She thought about it for a while, then realised it would be cheaper to do the degree than keep taking short courses. As her confidence grew, she gave up her job as a coder. In fact, she went through a complete career change, choosing instead to follow her bliss. She went from working in large companies doing mainly technical jobs to establishing a career within sustainable fashion in 2004.

Bushra went on to do another part-time degree with the coolest name – applied imagination, a branch of design studies. One of her projects was an interactive social benefit project that looked at memory and music, with music as the trigger for memory. The big idea at the time was to collect a kind of database of what music people were into, what smells they really responded to and what images they react with. Collecting all these pieces of data so that if they were in hospital and they'd lost their memory or were suffering from a neurodegenerative disease which had taken away a patient's sense of self, we'd be able to use what we'd collected to trigger their memory, or even their sense of self.

Although she didn't take the project any further, she could see how the others have used the data that's collected about all of us to sell us advertising. But just think, it could also be used to reunite us with our sense of self should we ever lose that.

More innovative projects followed as FOMO (fear of missing out) propelled Bushra to exciting things happening in new fields, which led to many different careers. As well as setting up her own creative studio, she's looked at improving VR headsets, used in gaming, and playing around with how they touch our skin. Her curiosity about wearable tech has led her to look at the ways in which haptics – something that gives the user touch-based feedback to their actions in VR – could be embedded into costumes, improving the experience of the story in a game through the garment. And, when used in conjunction with the VR headset, the whole experience is a spectacle, mixing up the sense of self through the wearer's sensory perception.

Bushra doesn't let the grass grow under her feet. Boredom fills her with more fear and dread than tackling something new. She's even become a part-time special constable. Bushra kicks butt.

Hours spent daydreaming as a child have fed Bushra's imagination, developed very strong visualisation skills and continues the expansion of her mind to this day. As a result of her broad interests, she finds herself making connections and seeing patterns, waking up in the middle of the night with an idea that is either a desire to fulfil a childhood dream, or she'll have a eureka moment that acts as an inspiration that helps to solve a problem she's been sweating over.

One of Bushra's favourite things to do is to draw, which she finds deeply meditative. She's fully present but lost in the moment, and that leads to some of her best ideas. The realisation of those ideas is through more research about the industry where the idea sits, digging for the 'how'. She'll look for someone who has pioneered something similar and read up on the path they took. Using transferable skills, she'll immerse herself in that industry, upskilling when required through online tutorials, meet-ups, adult education classes and experimenting in her studio. She believes that we are all creative, and that technology, which requires a high level of problem solving, is a way of expressing that creativity. But she's aware that we all carry

internal struggles, even within our own lanes.
For her it expresses itself this way . . .

> I am a creative coming from a science back-
> ground where there was a correct or wrong
> answer. It took a while for me to adjust and
> understand how to bear my creativity and be
> vulnerable and then fight for it. And the hard-
> est struggle has been that sometimes I've had
> to compromise my vision. Yes, the struggle is
> real, in a 'first world' sort of way, but to quote
> Maya Angelou, '. . . Still I rise'.

***Bushra's broad portfolio of interests is some-
thing we could all learn from.***

One of the things that stands out is that she
doesn't stick with just one arena, but all the
arenas feed each other and open her up. So we
could take a leaf from Bushra books and . . .

### Mix it up!

Bushra threw conventional out the window.
From her first degree she put two things together
that don't normally go together. Biochemistry
and management. It's like eating savoury and
sweet at the same time. And it worked for her.

### Use convention as just a guide.

You really can mix two things that shouldn't
really fit. Plus, it unlocks creativity. What two

things that excite you could you throw together to create a business you could start from your kitchen table? Creativity isn't just about art. Some people hear the word creativity and think, they don't have a creative bone in their body. But it takes creative thinking to create new ways of organising data, or recognising patterns helpful for analysis.

Bushra shows us that mixing it up and following our bliss are valid ways of earning a living. Try the mash-up! You've got nothing to lose. And you will definitely have fun. Take risks. Never stop learning. They say, look before you leap. True, because at our age we don't want to be breaking any bones. Look before you leap, but leap.

Whether you decide to go back to uni or to your local further education college to try something new, going back to school keeps the synapses firing and the curiosity fired up. Further education is not only a place to learn something new, it's also a great place to meet new people who share your interests. Hey, you could even meet someone you could end up starting a business with. If we hadn't been two of the oldest gals on that NFTS course, we'd never be writing this book together.

LIKE TROUBLES, A RISK SHARED IS A
RISK HALVED.

It means there's someone to talk to who's going through the same things you are. Someone to send cake and coffee when exhaustion and menopause hit at the same time. And best of all, someone there to celebrate with when the business starts to take off.

### FOLLOW YOUR BLISS.

Some of the most sustainable small businesses are built on what people love to do. What do you love doing that you could make a business out of? If you can't think of anything off the top of your head, have a few friends over. Break out the coffee, tea and cakes. Sometimes our friends see parts of us that we can't see. Get them to make lists of things you're really good at. Provide them with paper, pens and stickers – make it fun. Get them all to vote to find the top three.

Before you throw all their ideas out, take a long hard look at them. Sometimes we dismiss ideas because we think they're too foolish, or because we're afraid because no one has ever done it before. Just sit with them for a while. Your friends could be right. There just might be a business in that thing you love that you think is weird.

Whether you decide to build a new business, begin a new career or learn something new, what's important is to make sure we earn enough to ensure we have some time to relax at the end. We can't undervalue ourselves. The bravest thing we have to do is ask for a decent wage.

*'Ask for the highest amount you can say out loud
without actually laughing.'*

– Cindy Gallop

You may not believe it, but we have a duty to demand as much as we can get. We have the power to significantly change the gender pay gap. Especially in this world of alternative facts, where the current figures can be interpreted in ways that make the gender pay gap the world's biggest problem or almost non-existent. But when you look at the disparity in women's lifetime income, no one can argue that women pay a hefty price for ensuring the world is populated.

Some companies are accidentally creating a greater divide. By bringing in young women on starting salaries they're widening the inequity. No wonder the World Economic Forum says we're 202 years from parity on the global gender pay gap. Bringing older women back into the workforce and compensating them well would solve the problem much quicker.

When people talk of the wage gap they usually focus on low-income earners, but the figures are horrendous at the top. In 2019, men earning over £150,000 outnumbered women 5:1 and 10 times more make over a million. And of the 2,153 billionaires across the world, only 252 are women, and only 3 are Black women. It's easy to see that the problem needs to be solved at all levels.

One thing's for sure, sensible businesses will invest heavily in older women if they genuinely want to survive. Even now there are more people aged over 65 than there are children under 5. You don't have to be Einstein to realise we can't afford for the majority of our population to lie idle. We need to get a new narrative out there – in a world where humanity will be the most valuable business tool – we need to be selling ourselves and the unique talents we bring.

Wisdom and experience make a winning combination. And it's nothing new – great footballers don't die, they become great managers and lead their young, fit teams to victory using strategies honed over decades. Same in politics; the newcomers on the US political scene appear to have wisdom beyond their years because they have wisdom on their teams. Seasoned campaigners and civil rights activists advise the bright-eyed new members of Congress and it shows. They are polished, informed and have a passion that has lived since Martin Luther King, Jr, stood at that bridge in Selma.

Let's cross new bridges side by side and create a new working future.

A future that works for all of us.

# 18

# INVEST

### *It's time to put our money where our future is*

June 2020

> CAROL
>
> I can eat! I don't have to choose
> between food and toilet paper.

> JANE
>
> You can get toilet paper?

> CAROL
>
> No, but I got something rarer - a job
> in the middle of a pandemic.

> JANE
>
> How come?

> CAROL
>
> My mate's business has just taken off
> and the work's rolling in!

Has it sunk in yet how powerful we are? Well let's take it to the next level. Some of us are going to struggle during Covid recovery, some are going to make a mint and most will just have enough to get by. But what if we could thrive? All we have to do is invest in each other.

The first steps are easy; got a friend who needs a job? Keep your ear out. If you're working, have a chat to HR on their behalf or scroll through the jobs vacant on your LinkedIn profile. Be her champion, recommend her – stick your neck out! And if she's starting up a business, tell everyone you know, buy her products or services at full price then show them off on social media. You'd be amazed how powerful personal recommendations are for new businesses, especially tiny ones.

There will be a lot of people who need work or support with new ventures in the next few years, nobody should feel like a victim. Start using your spending power and powerful multi-generational networks to invest in the people you believe in. In 2019, out of $104 billion in venture capital funding only 2.2% went to women, and women of colour received less than 1% (which is ridiculous when they are the fastest-growing group of new entrepreneurs). We can't find these figures broken down for age, but we can only assume investment in older women's businesses hovers somewhere around the zero mark.

The current startup culture is all based around finding 'unicorns' – imaginary beasts with a value of $1 billion. Yet a hell of a lot of women start businesses simply to feed their families or enrich their communities. They might not have big ideas that will change the world, they're usually things that make your life a little better. And they're local. Buy the spice kit from the woman in your town, or her candles. Now we've been forced to stay at home, we've discovered what treasures are right on our doorstep. Keep buying them.

There are a lot of people who are actively working to create new systems and investment structures to open opportunities for midlife women because up until now we haven't fared well in the bro-startup culture where it seems only pretty young white women get funded (at a paltry percentage of what the bros get). We're not pretty – beautiful, attractive, handsome, yes – and we're not girls. We're not afraid to say what we think. Which can be scary to bullish investors who are used to calling the shots.

> *'Time and trouble will tame an advanced young woman, but an advanced old woman is uncontrollable by any earthly force.'*
>
> – Dorothy L. Sayers

The simple fact is – and it's been demonstrated perfectly during the various lockdowns – if you can run a family, you can run a small business. And there's a tribe of superwomen out there who can do so much more. Any woman who has run a PTA could run a Fortune 500 company. Any woman who's been the treasurer could run the world. Alas, that doesn't read well on a CV, and the current job-seeking algorithm isn't designed to recognise our unique skills or search the keywords that truly describe us.

Let's create our own ways of investing in and employing each other. Starting by changing the ridiculous notion that motherhood is a career break into motherhood is a career enhancer with great value. If a 35-year-old man took a break at the height of his career to climb a mountain or explore the world, would he come back to a two-week training course and a minimum-wage internship? Motherhood is tougher than climbing any mountain and teaches you more than any exploration could. It should further your career. Not take it back to the beginning.

All the real-life data points to us being the ideal candidate for a multitude of roles and enterprises. A startup founded by someone over 50 is 2.2 times more likely to succeed than one founded by a 30-year-old. Any founder who is looking for a business advantage should look at those figures and then look for someone over 50 to give them an even bigger chance of success.

Anyone who wants to really fly should look for a woman over 50. Especially when research proves that women over 55 make the best bosses.

And yes, we know, nobody wants to work with their mum. But stop and think:

If you were a product, how well were you brought to market?

How much of your success do you accredit to her selfless devotion?

And how many times was she right?

Of course, most of us don't want to work with our actual mum. But what about a woman just like her? What do you get?

A negotiator – anyone who can get a seven-year-old to eat broccoli can persuade a client to do anything.

A doer. We know we have to do the 'unsexy' stuff. Seriously, one of the major reasons why older people succeed with their startups is they know the boring things like meticulous book-keeping, following legal counsel and having workable ethics and a long-term view are the cornerstones to success.

A budgeter. Invest in a midlife woman and she'll make it grow, not throw it away on fancies. A woman who has balanced a family budget knows the electric bills are paid before you buy toys. Foosball tables are not essential business equipment.

A time management expert. A woman who has run a family runs multiple diaries in her head, she knows where everyone is and where they should be. She makes sure everyone gets there and back on time and still finds time for herself.

A champion. At this time in our lives, we have achieved so much; it may be as simple as having raised healthy humans or we could have reached the glittering heights with awards coming out of our wazoo. Whichever end of the spectrum one sits on, the need for constant ego gratification lessens with age. We are quite happy to support younger people in their quest for world domination. But be warned, it will come with a healthy dose of devil's advocacy. All our experience alerts us to possible outcomes that seem impossible. But then the same applies to our ideas.

Especially in the world of tech. In a world that idolises digital natives, we overlook the women who taught them how to use a computer. And now the age tech market is worth $2 trillion, it makes little sense to ignore women with an innate understanding of what needs to be made to make old age better. One of the advantages of living longer means we get to spend more time with our parents and some of us are even lucky enough to have our grans around. We know what they need. We also know where they've come from and what they've experienced.

Our analogue talents are valuable too. What practical problems could you solve in this new world? Can you find new ways of introducing like-minded people when office romances are unlikely? Is there something you could create to save your high street? What could you provide that helps mums working from home?

Whether we're just getting by or on our way to wild success there's one person we all need to invest in, and that's ourselves. Many of us are embarrassed by our financial situation and there is no class divide to our shame. Many of us didn't handle our money as wisely as we should. But is it our fault?

The rise of women was seen as a huge opportunity by the rich white men in power. These con men had a whole generation of 'marks' who had almost zero financial education: we weren't expected to know about these sorts of things. Men were supposed to look after our financial security. We were never encouraged to save – quite the opposite, actually. When credit cards came out in the 1960s, they were shamelessly promoted to young women by ads with slogans like, 'All a girl needs when she goes out shopping,' accompanied by an image of a woman with a Barclaycard tucked into a bikini. But even if she were paying the bill, she had to get her husband or father's permission to get the card in the first place.

To the men who ran the world when we were younger, our careers were only a bit of fun until we found a man. They believed our salaries should be frittered away in that endeavour – at an astonishingly high-interest rate.

If we did find our 'man', we never got the message to manage our own finances. Housewives were just spending machines and their purchases the butt of every working men's club comedian's jokes. If we worked, we had to take unpaid leave to have kids and many early career women spent all of their salary on childcare. Let's not forget, a quarter of us ended up as single mums. You can raise kids and run a house on one salary but there's unlikely to be anything left to save or invest. And many single mums rely on housing benefit. As soon as the kids turn 18 that stops. Then where do they go?

Even the women who were prudent and made wise saving decisions are recalibrating. Energetic women with private pensions are hitting 65 and discovering all their hard work will only keep them living to their current standard for 10 years, if they're lucky.

And women who planned their whole working life around retiring at 60 have to work another seven years before they get the benefits they've contributed to their whole working lives – if they keep their job. Because laying off a woman in midlife is the ultimate bastard act of the patriarchy. And they know it. In 2019, NatWest stationed actors at the entrance to tube stations all over London armed with bunches of roses. They apologised to women for the appalling way that banks have patronised us in the past.

We don't need *patronising* apologies. In fact, we really don't need anything. When we invest in each other, we build profitable companies, services and products that benefit our communities and provide women like us with well-paid work. If we build businesses and services that provide empathetic and realistic financial advice and products that can help us save, we will be able to build a better retirement for ourselves and a better world for future generations.

# 19

# INTERLUDE

## *It's a long journey – take your time*

We know, you're tired and your knees may be a bit dodgy. The thought of getting up and changing the world is probably exhausting, but we have to lead by example. And that means looking after ourselves, eating well and getting enough shut-eye – even if it is at 3 pm. There's little use to us re-entering the workforce if we don't make some positive changes. The health benefits of a 20-minute nap are well-documented. You could start a trend – the art of the disco nap.

We could start a lot of trends. Slowing down would be a good place to start.

Our empirical understanding of the passage of time can have a soothing effect on every environment we inhabit. Our well-earned experience of how long things really take can help everyone take a few deep breaths and slow down.

Because we've learnt the hard way that rash decisions rarely pan out, immediate gratification doesn't last and most problems can be solved by a good night's sleep.

We're the front runners in the new marathon of longer lives.

We need to pace ourselves. When the world is moving so quickly, it's our job to encourage everyone to take some time and consider the road ahead.

## 20

# INNOVATE

## *It's a whole new world that needs new things*

September 2018

> JANE
>
> I mentored at the teens in AI hackathon.

> CAROL
>
> Say that again in English.

> JANE
>
> It's where teens, techies and mentors come together to work out real world problems and build an artificial intelligence prototype over the weekend.

> CAROL
>
> What sort of real world problems?

> JANE
>
> Well get this, a woman from the NHS set one of the tasks as how to get

```
          men to send bowel cancer tests back.
          Apparently they will stick a swab up
      ,   their bum but are too embarrassed to
          pop it in the post.

                        CAROL
          And what was the solution?

                        JANE
          Dunno. The teens weren't the slightest
          bit interested. They all answered the
          fake news task.
```

Even before Covid, we were living in a new world that needs new tech – and doing it without the input of brilliant women who'd know exactly where to tell men to stick their anal swabs.

None of us really knows how the world will end up. It's changing. And change brings myriad opportunities. Especially for those of us who are used to dealing with it.

The pandemic has altered forever the way the world shops, communicates, does business and treats each other.

Things are going to get a lot more local: what can you build to better serve your community?

Who got left behind in the old normal? What can you build to help them?

People have changed. Their needs have changed. Their desires have changed. So, in this new world, what can we offer to satisfy this new market?

New businesses are sprouting up all over the world and the internet is the marketplace. So, should we think big? Amazon and Apple both started in garages. Or small? Thousands of stories abound of women's businesses started from the kitchen table.

## Dame Stephanie Shirley

When Stephanie Shirley butted her head against the glass ceiling, it was made of concrete. She lost her patience, quit her job overnight, got the necessary permission from her husband to open a business bank account and started a social enterprise. Of course, there wasn't a term for such a business back then. There was also no such thing as professional working mothers.

It was 1962, just 17 years after the end of the Second World War, where computing had taken its early steps. Alan Turing and his team at Bletchley Park, England, commissioned and operated the Colossus, the world's first programmable, electronic digital computer; 75% of the early programmers and operators were women. And there were a lot of them: 8,000 women worked at Bletchley at all levels during the war. They proved that women could not only work in a man's world but thrive and innovate in it. However, after the war, the female pioneers of early computing were kept hidden by the Official Secrets Act. What's more, professional women were expected to abandon their careers once pregnant and there was no return.

Stephanie started her software company Freelance Programmers as a crusade for these women. Minute number one in the company's annals stated that it shall be company policy to provide jobs for women with children. This quickly changed to 'careers' for women with children because Stephanie also started the business with a flash of insight.

At the time, everyone was enamoured with computer hardware, but she believed software was the way of the future. And she was right. Her female team took on leading-edge projects from scheduling the national railways to developing the black box for the supersonic Concorde.

Her company, Freelance Programmers, was a radical company run by radical feminists. And it worked. Or rather, collaborated:

> There was a great sense of flexibility, I could help you, Jane, in the morning, Carol could help me in the afternoon. It was a team working, it was collegiate. We liked each other as people as well as working together. I found manageri-ally I got on much better and had better results when I showed my vulnerabilities. Somehow men don't do that. All the sort of questions that I, and doubtless other women, ask are viewed as ignorance rather than a desire for knowl-edge. The company had a very feminine feel to it – and very professional – we really bent over backwards to make sure that our systems were right, our response times were right and that we looked right.

This meant an informal dress code that excluded trousers. This may seem to us to go against everything the firm stood for, but these women were still operating in a 'man's' world where women in trousers were seen as threatening. Letters from women were also rarely answered. Despairing that Stephanie's new business drive – which consisted of sending personal letters to the heads of industry every week – wasn't yielding the results she expected, her husband suggested she use her family nickname to sign her new business letters. Steve Shirley became the new tech bro in town.

Forty-five years after losing her patience with the patriarchy, the company she founded (now part of the SopraSteria group) had a revenue of almost $3 billion and employed 8,500 people; 60% were women. The 1975 Sex Discrimination Act made her women-only operation illegal so she had to employ men too (if they were good enough!). When Dame Stephanie (a title she rightly earned in 2000) left her crusading female company in 1993, she was irked that the gender make-up of the boardroom didn't reflect the gender balance of the workforce. Most of the top jobs were taken by men. It seemed the work of the suffragettes, the valiant working heroines of the Second World War and the second-wave feminists had only made a crack in the glass ceiling.

'I hope young women don't give up hope or get depressed that it's taking so long. It doesn't surprise me,' she said, 'real cultural change takes time. Fifty years is nothing in the scheme of things.'

At 87, Dame Stephanie Shirley enjoys a glorious view from a great height. When she was younger, she had the ability to look at a whole mass of figures and, without analysing, be able to determine that 'There's something funny over there in that part.' Like the Bletchley code-breakers before her, she had the rare talent of pattern recognition. Add a lifetime of experience and truly beautiful patterns arrive. When she welcomed nervous and guilty parents to Prior's Court, the school she had lovingly founded in 1999, and now a centre of excellence for children with autism, she knew how hard it was for devoted parents to place their trust and precious child in the hands of strangers. She had done exactly the same with her beautiful son Giles when he became too strong to look after at home. So she used her dotcom boom fortune to create the environment she wished had existed when he had needed it.

At this precise moment a bigger pattern revealed itself to her. The worst thing that ever happened in her life made complete sense. In 1939, five-year-old Vera Stephanie Buchtal was loaded on a train in Vienna to escape the Nazis. Her mother had to trust that the kindness of strangers would give her daughter a chance at life. What had felt like abandonment for most of her life turned into the greatest gift she ever received. One she could pass on.

*Some lessons we can all learn from how Dame Stephanie ran her business 59 years ago:*

Don't be afraid to speak your own language
and build on your experience.

When Dame Stephanie recruited women to program computers she equated it with knitting
patterns. If you could make a perfectly fitted
jumper from pages of simple instructions like
k2, p2 (knit two stitches, purl two stitches), you
could easily program software. Hiring people
with transferable skills and training them is
cost-effective and promotes better representation of all groups in the workforce. Give people
the opportunity to change their own lives and
your business will always be a success.

You are in the business of making money and
the image you project must sell.

In the 1960s, feminism was all the rage, in the
1970s it was perceived as a threat. Freelance
Programmers carved a place for itself because
it was 'groovy' – it even featured on *Tomorrow's
World*. But in the seventies its women needed to
be better than the men – but the men didn't need
to know it was women beating them. The image
projected was of a progressive software company. By the time the company was floated on the
Stock Exchange in 1996, the only clue to the feminist empire was the fact it was born of a queen.

In the beginning Dame Stephanie expected her
workers would stay for about seven years (the
hard yards of motherhood) – many stayed for
twenty. These days, when tech companies turn-
over the best staff in a matter of months, creating

a stable culture that respects experience will attract and keep the best people. Remember that all businesses are people businesses.

### Work religiously on your sales pipeline.

Dame Stephanie scoured the papers and her networks for the names of the men (it was always men) she could do business with. Every week she would sit down and draft a personal letter to each one with a solid argument as to why he should employ Freelance Programmers and what benefits the company could bring. These days there are plenty of ways to research and network your sales targets and myriad ways of communicating. However you decide to make that 'cold call', making it personal warms it up.

### Starting a company using an invisible workforce gives you the pick of the best.

The women who answered Dame Stephanie's ads (and were lucky enough to have access to a phone – a rarity in the early 1960s) learnt life-long and valuable skills and 70 of them exhibited leadership abilities that made them millionaires. What invisible workforce could you turn into multi-millionaires?

### You're the boss.

In the early days of the company when her son was small, Dame Stephanie only had a babysitter on a Tuesday afternoon. Therefore she only

took meetings on a Tuesday afternoon. It's
your business; you set the timetable. Make it
work for you.

## MONEY ISN'T EVERYTHING.

The business was not founded to make money, it
was founded to employ women, which meant it
succeeded straight away. It was 25 years before
it paid a dividend. There is a simple explanation
for this: Dame Stephanie was a woman ahead
of her time. Bill Gates started Microsoft in his
garage 13 years after she started hers from her
kitchen table. They both turned a profit at about
the same time. When you know you have a good
idea, stick with it. Sometimes it takes time for
the world to catch up with you.

If you went to any new business forums over the last few
years you would see lots of women starting businesses.
Usually, they are:

- Beauty creams
- Spice kits
- Candles

In the old model, the vast majority of these women would
end up after years of hard work and stress with nothing more
than a garage filled with beauty creams, spice kits, candles or
stock from multi-level marketing companies.

Nobody really helped them. There was money to be made

from business loans, training courses and marketing campaigns disguised as new business accelerators to show how much big companies care about small business. But these business accelerators offered months-long programmes with mentorship, office space and supply chain resources that are usually in big cities and operated from nine to five. Many women starting a business stop working when their kids come home from school or start when they go to bed. Usually both. They didn't need mentoring by young people looking for the next unicorn; they needed help to make a decent living in the hours that work for them.

Now money's tight, the big companies will care more about small crumbs and the clever ones will take micro-businesses more seriously. Especially when we really invest in each other and support the small businesses that are designed to keep a roof overhead and food on the table.

But there is one new business venture we should avoid like the plague: 81% of business coaches fail.

No wonder women had garages filled with dead stock. We had failing businesses helping businesses that never stood a chance. And then there are whole industries built to take advantage of our money, time and dreams.

Like creative writing courses. They're filled to overflowing with mature women. Yes, we've all got a book in us. Or a film. Or a twelve-part TV series. But let's get real. Few are going to make it. The Writer's Guild of America has around 20,000 members but only 2,188 screenwriters got paying work in 2019. Why on earth would you train to join an industry where most of the current workers are already unemployed?

Yes, your story's great and you could be the one in a million who are going to make it. Miracles happen. But don't count on it. If you have the time to spare, mastering a new skill and expressing yourself is a valuable life experience. But it's highly unlikely to give you anything more than a manuscript in your bottom drawer.

But what else are we hiding in there? We really have to stop looking at what we'd like to do and start looking at what we can give. But most of all we've got to follow the money.

Age tech is coming and will be one of the most highly invested arenas of the digital age. It's all about digitally enabling the longevity economy. In other words, the tech industry has worked out we're living longer and they're looking for more ways to make money from us. Seriously? If ever there was a time for us to be starting up shop, it's now.

We've got to lead the longevity economy and take advantage of our wisdom and our years. We need to own age tech. After all, it's for us. And it's not that difficult. We just have to turn our minds to creating new businesses with ideas for services purchased by older people, purchased on behalf of older people, traded between older and younger people or delivered to future older people. Or look for a job in the sector because any startup that wants to sell to us that doesn't employ us is almost certainly destined to fail.

A healthy combination of old school and *nu skool* is the most sensible way to create the future. An age-neutral environment where all experience is valued is essential for the future of age tech. Because no matter how smart, or how much bravado younger people possess, there are no shortcuts to the second half of life. You have to put in the hard yards to get to this point in the road. They can't possibly see everything ahead, when they're so far behind.

# 21

# INITIATE

*Start something. Anything.*

February 2020

> CAROL
>
> We've had two takers.

> JANE
>
> Is this your theatre project?

> CAROL
>
> Yes. And I've got the two theatres
> I wanted.

> JANE
>
> Yay, *Raised Voices* is finally
> happening!

> CAROL
>
> We've got six writers, two theatres and
> the first bit of funding and you know
> what that means?

> JANE
>
> Money follows money?

CAROL

**And women over 45 are going to take over the world.**

It's not just about building businesses and bolstering the economy. If we've learnt anything from these times, it's the importance of people and quality of life.

We were all in lockdown together and a higher station in life offered no magical protection from the coronavirus, but it gave everyone a greater appreciation of those who kept the country running with a lot less protection than our four walls provided. Some midlife women are very, very comfortable with a lot of time on their hands. Get uncomfortable and do something that will help those who maybe haven't had the same advantages, opportunities, education or luck as you. Start with your local food bank – it's usually in a local church over afternoon tea one day a week or a drop-in centre. Why not drop in with teabags and a jumbo bag of tampons? You may be lucky enough to sit with some of the women there, and learn that life can turn on a sixpence. Even the most passionate atheist would leave with a 'there by the grace of God go I!'

Don't go as a saviour, go as an ally, this isn't time to give charity (although it's time when we all need to give to charity); it's time to build opportunities. Meet the women who are suffering, discover what they need more than a plastic bag of groceries. And build it. Or become part of already growing grassroots movements, help not-for-profit organisations or just volunteer where you can.

Or simply, help our kids. The Parkland Kids and Greta Thunberg have made a huge splash on the world stage. The younger generation may have the ideas and the confidence to send out a powerful message in front of the camera, but behind them there are women with a tremendous amount of business, PR, legal wisdom, who love driving them, often literally.

We can all start something even if it's just a new conversation. The last few years have seen us all divided like never before which is ridiculous when we are connected like never before.

We left something very valuable behind:

*The world faces a deficit of social imagination.*
*We find it easy to imagine apocalypse and disaster;*
*or to imagine new generations of technology. But*
*we find it much harder than in the past to imagine*
*a better society a generation or more into the future.*
*There are many possible reasons for this decline;*
*loss of confidence in progress and grand narratives;*
*declining imaginative capacity; slowing down*
*of innovation. Key institutions – universities,*
*political parties and think tanks – have for*
*different reasons vacated this space. The decline of*
*imagination matters because societies need a wide*
*range of ideas and options to help them adjust,*
*particularly to big challenges like*
*climate change and ageing.*

Geoff Mulgan, April 2020

We have everything we need to spur the social imagination. No one can deny the necessity of social networks while we were all apart. Our reach spans multiple generations across the globe. Connections are vital. Use them. Spread goodness. Share our dreams for the future.

Instead of spewing outrage, let's start conversations and

share visions. If you read an article or blog that spurs your imagination, instead of just posting it, research around it then post it with your personal take. Or better still, write your own article. Because the constant attack on 'fake news' has made even the most respected of sources redundant to someone who gets their news from the other side of the political divide, a *Telegraph* reader will ignore anything featured in the *Guardian* and vice-versa. If we're going to have conversations about the things we care about and can actually do something about, the only way to change minds is to remove imaginary boundaries. Right or Left, we all want a better world. When we don't trust sources, let's trust the opinions of people we know and love and put some real, well-researched truth out there in our own words. If others share different views, instead of dismissing them out of hand try looking at them with curiosity, put our scepticism to the side and keep our feelings in check to learn where those beliefs came from, even if we'll never understand where they ended up. When we see falsehoods let's put them right with reasoned argument. But don't hang around when trolls are striking: some opinions are so entrenched that nothing will stop them.

Except maybe this: when you have made your final point, say, 'But I am sure you will want the final word on this.' There really is no come back for that.

Of course, we don't all have to start conversations. Sometimes the comments on a post reveal so much more than the original intended. If you come in and ask genuine questions the answers from friends of friends or contacts of contacts can be revelations. Connect with them too. When we expand our media bubbles it opens us up to new ideas and viewpoints.

Prior to Covid, everyone was worried that we were all stuck in these bubbles. Then they were replaced by our own four walls. For many this has brought great loneliness, mental health trauma and family discord. We really do need to imagine a way out of this for all of us.

*'Younger people tend to put walls up to their own creativity. You don't need to do that, the world puts up the walls.'*

Mara Marich

Let's not confine ourselves with what is. Let's start making things to make things better. Up until now it appeared the only way of getting around walls was either climbing over them or smashing them down. How about we leave them exactly where they are? Decorate them and build something new around them? Create a window?

As much as we'd like to think the patriarchy can be dismantled gently and in an orderly fashion, we really need to cover all our bases. We're all very different kinds of women and it would be pretty sad if we all joined together and all we built was a boring new stereotype. Let's use all our ammunition and attack on all fronts.

Some who were ahead of their time have fought lonely battles. They haven't asked politely for change. They've demanded it. Those who play by the rules have to give space to those who colour outside of the lines. We need to let the artists, the mad women, and the mad as hell women smash a few walls if they want to. If nothing else, we have shared experience.

In 1976, whether we were nice girls or rebels, punk had an effect on those of us who were teenagers at the time, most of it extremely negative. The cool, sanitised modern 'Brit Punk' graphics of today hide a seriously scary subculture in a scary time. The 1970s was a violent place, especially with the rise of the National Front in Britain and the fear of the terrorism of the IRA. There was racism fuelled by skinheads, punks and football hooligans. There were strikes and power cuts and a three-day week. Britain was not a happy place.

But the music was cool. And the fashion was radical. It was an artists' playground. Like the psychedelic 1960s, the anarchy of the 1970s was groovy, baby. A world that fetishises youth is turning its back on the generations who created pop culture. When Bowie left this planet, the digital natives googled him to death; we'd been along for the ride since 'The Laughing Gnome'.

Those of us with a visceral understanding of pop culture and time have a duty to shout our thoughts and talents and creations from the rooftops.

> *'Oh yeah, we're supposed to disappear into the woods. Fuck that!'*
>
> Neneh Cherry

Especially when Mick Jagger is seen as a god, but rock goddesses are expected to quietly disappear.

Oh yeah, it's time to scream like Siouxie and the Banshees!

Those of us with a voice need to use it.

Those with megaphones need to turn them up to 11.

... Especially the few rare female souls who seem to have had their 'couldn't give a fuck' on from birth. These women have always challenged the norm, and their lives have led them to brush with true genius. Let them smash down as many damned walls as they like, but let's try and make it a bit easier for them this time.

## Sinéad O'Connor

On 3 October 1992, a beautiful young woman with a shaved head, wearing a simple white lace dress, stood in front of a microphone, a table of candles to her side. She took a big deep breath and her angelic Irish voice filled the room with the words Haile Selassie, the final Emperor of Ethiopia, had delivered to the United Nations in 1963. She sang as if his ancestor Makeda was questioning the world once more.

*Until the philosophy*
*Which hold one race superior and another*
*Inferior*
*Is finally*
*And permanently*
*Discredited*
*And abandoned*
*Everywhere is war*
*Me say war*

Sinéad O'Connor, the wild punk, who toned it down and gained fame as the bald-headed girl who cried straight to camera sweetly singing Prince's 'Nothing Compares 2 U', gave the audience exactly what they came to see. And what the producers expected – in dress rehearsals Sinéad had carried a photograph of a refugee child to illustrate the song and ensure the perfect camera angle.

But as the *Saturday Night Live* cameras rolled Sinéad made the song her own. She expanded the war to include a new battle against the sexual exploitation of children within the Catholic Church. It was personal. She was a victim herself; as a teenager she had been abused at a Magdalene Laundry run by the church. Her vocals were angry and pointed and in perfect pitch. She was bewitching.

As she sang the word 'evil' she held up a picture of Pope John Paul then tore it up, threw the pieces at the camera and said, 'Fight the real enemy'.

There was deathly silence from the audience. Sinéad just shrugged, took out her earphones, blew out the candles and walked off stage.

Next week on *Saturday Night Live*, Joe Pesci, a good Italian Catholic, opened the show with the picture taped back together saying, 'If it were my show I'd have given her such a smack.'

That was the least of the abuse, the vicious attack by the media turned the vulnerable woman with the angelic voice into the devil incarnate. The next two decades would see her life subjected to a constant glare of hate, an imposition that became too much. Sinéad's mental health issues became very public, each episode met with a new name and another set of meds and every personal problem exacerbated by tabloids filled with lies.

It never mattered what the world wanted to say about Sinéad, she always had a way of sharing her truth: her music. Sinéad has released ten studio albums since 1987 that tell her life story in every line. Yet she is still defined by one chapter. Even though Pope John Paul finally admitted there was child sexual abuse in the Catholic Church, the messenger had already been shot. Or had she?

When asked by *Salon* magazine in 2002 if she would change anything about the SNL appearance, Sinéad said, 'Hell, no!', and in a 2010 op-ed for the *Washington Post* she said,

'I knew my action would cause trouble, but I wanted to force a conversation where there was a need for one; that is part of being an artist. All I regretted was that people assumed I didn't believe in God.'

Anyone who has listened to Sinéad's music can have no doubt of her belief. Her journey running from the spotlight became a quest for enlightenment that saw her study various religious practices all across the world, she even became a priest in the Orthodox Catholic and Apostolic Church for a while. But now it seems she's found a faith and a name that feels right for her. Islam.

In September 2019, Shuhada Sadaqat shared an intimate and searing version of the song that made her famous. Watching her sing 'Nothing Compares 2 U' on live TV wearing a red burkah and accompanied by a string section was as bewitching as her SNL performance twenty-seven years before. It was haunting to hear a woman sing her anthem after the patriarchy almost destroyed her. The power of hearing her beautiful voice singing, 'I know that living with you baby was sometimes hard' holds layers of meaning that can only come with the passage of time.

Time that keeps on moving, in October 2020 she released a cover of gospel singer and civil rights activist Mahalia Jackson's 'Trouble of the World' which features the lyrics.

*Soon I will be done*
*With the trouble of the world*
*Trouble of the world*
*Trouble of the world.*

When we all start looking at what we can do to tackle the trouble of the world to make a better future for our children maybe we should be asking:

### What can we do to make a better world for Sinéad O'Connor?

Only a tiny fraction of the women reading this book will have the passion, conviction and spotlight to confront uncomfortable truths so powerfully to a world that doesn't want to change, but all of us who experience wrongdoing have the right to speak of it – even if it's only to a close friend.

Your lived experience is your truth. Sinéad experienced trauma, she never disguised it and she never hid it. She knew she wasn't alone. She also knew that it was heresy to criticise the structure that had enabled and protected her abuser. She stated her truth and took the barrage of hate she expected. Then continued to live her truth till the world caught up.

Many who are conceived as mad are simply

ahead of their time. Today Sinéad's performance wouldn't shock: everyone knows the Catholic Church has been hiding its paedophilia problem for decades and is now trying to clean up its act. The word is out. And a whisper network of damaged children got a beautiful bullhorn in Sinéad, who used her spotlight to shine a light on their pain.

To the media-led public, she was a troubled woman bouncing around in a world she didn't belong in. But there was a world she will always be at home in. The music industry. A quick glance at her discography shows a musical journey as comprehensive as her spiritual quest working with artists around the globe from Willie Nelson to Jah Wobble. Even when the whole world feels as though it is working against you, there will always be people who feel the same and respect your talent. Keep these people close, they will keep you real and keep you going even through the hardest of times.

Be patient and if you're not that virtuous, be tenacious – both produce exactly the same result. When we face a no it's not always a no, sometimes it's a not now. Many women with new ideas get frustrated that the world doesn't change quickly enough. Those who already see a world that was inconceivable to us as teenagers know different – we know change is constant and happens faster than you realise.

# 22

# INTERVENE

## *Standing up for what we believe in*

October 2019

> JANE
>
> Fuck, I'm loving *Watchmen*.

> CAROL
>
> Good innit.

> JANE
>
> But what I want to know is why am I
> first hearing about the Tulsa massa-
> cre from a comic book TV series?

> CAROL
>
> Because you don't read.

> JANE
>
> It's not been in anything I've
> ever read.

> CAROL
>
> I know, we've read all your stuff. You
> haven't read ours. African American

```
fiction's been telling us all this
for years. Have you ever touched
Audre Lorde, Zora Neale Hurston,
Toni Morrison?

                  JANE
I read Toni. As for the others, it's the
first time I'm hearing their names.

                  CAROL
Of course it is. No one ever told you
about our writers, no one thought
you'd be interested. We lapped them up.
The only books you people read are
books we write talking about why we
don't talk to you.
```

In the early days of the internet and social media, we were truly excited that mass communication was giving us an opportunity to gather together in virtual tribes. Who knew it would turn into *Lord of the Flies* so quickly? In William Golding's 1951 novel, it only takes a matter of weeks for the boys to get naked, smear their faces in paint, appoint the 'natural leader, (the tallest, most handsome and sociopathic boy) then descend into a spiral of violence. Of course, we should have known the division of us all on social media would have the same result. Patriarchal stories have always been filled with tales about the 'darkness of a man's heart'. And it's complete and utter codswallop.

In 1965, six boys, fed up with the food and bored to death at their Tongan boarding school stole a fishing boat and sailed off. They were caught in a storm. Fifteen months later an Australian accountant, escaping the boredom of his family business, noticed a fire on a deserted island; he stopped his fishing boat and a wild creature with hair to his waist climbed

aboard followed by five other lost boys. They were well fed,
healthy and getting along with each other just fine.

As Captain Peter Warner said, 'By the time we arrived,
the boys had set up a small commune with food garden,
hollowed-out tree trunks to store rainwater, a gymnasium
with curious weights, a badminton court, chicken pens and
a permanent fire, all from handiwork, an old knife blade and
much determination.'

The boys didn't fight, they built a guitar and sang. When
one of them broke their leg, they didn't abandon him – they
set it. They didn't get distracted and let the fire go out. They
knew that was their only hope of rescue.

So, don't let the fire go out. This is time for our truth and
the power of our tribe.

Believe it or not, people will listen to us because we're not
seen as threatening. Those with violently differing views are
less likely to attack because they have experience of being
ticked off by a mother figure. Imagine the power of all of us
giving the world a gentle scolding with a lot of love? It's time for
more cups of tea – or a nice rack of ribs. A group of dedicated
midlife women can do anything if they put their minds to it.
And every little bit helps, like this wonderful Tumblr exchange:

Tumblr guy #1

*I was eating dinner with my mum and when she went to pay I
noticed a 'Hooters' frequent diner card or whatever in her wallet.
I asked her WTF, and she explained that a friend of hers got a
coupon for the grand opening and so a group of them went for lunch
just to try it out. This is a group that consists of women from their
50s into their 80s. Apparently, the food was decent but the service
was amazing, and the servers were 'all such wonderful girls, so
sweet! Said it was nice to take a break from all the gross men they
had to deal with' So they decided to come back. Now they go once*

*a week at least, and the Hooters waitresses fight each other for who
gets to serve them. Anyhow, I thought it was cute.*

Tumblr guy #2

*I'm all for the idea of a bunch of aunties and grandmas invading a
space typically dominated by men acting like gross creepers and just
taking the fuck over and being nice to the ladies on staff.*

*Because who the fuck is going to argue with an army of polite
older ladies?*

*Nobody, that's who.*

If you want to make the world a nicer place, take your joy
and empathy to places where it's rarely seen. There's great
strength in numbers and what could seem scary to a solo
midlife woman becomes a marvellous adventure for a group.
Especially when there's wine involved.

Or tear gas. At the start of the Black Lives Matter protests
the mums of America united like never before. Watching it
unfold on Twitter was a real-time demonstration of our power.

*woman 1*

*heyoooo!! I'm a fatass 39 year old mom and I got gassed for the
first time tonight when this happened. I was wearing a fucking ann
taylor loft blouse and everything (no like for real). how do you do,
youths! I'll be back with all the neighborhood moms! LOVED IT.*

*woman 2*

*I'm a fatass 57 year old arthritic mom. Been out in the protests
in Seattle since I was tear gassed in late May. Moms are going to
take down the police corruption and this awful, horrible president.
apparently the moms are organizing on facebook so if you're on there
look for a 'wall of moms' event happening tonight!!*

*woman 3*

*Welcome aboard!! I'm a fatass 56 year old mom who got gassed by Seattle cops on May 30 while nonviolently protesting. The gas is no fun, but didn't stop me from going back to more protests.*

*Also – I was only at the front of the line because a Black sister asked white folks to be their shield. Listen to them and follow their lead!*

They certainly followed their lead. They started out as a small Facebook group of predominantly white middle-class mums – when they captured the world's imagination they quickly changed the admins to Black women who had been fighting this fight for a damned sight longer.

When one of them had the bright idea of bringing a leaf blower to send back the tear gas fired at protestors, the dads stepped up to the plate to do 'their job' and built a wall in front of the mums.

And when veterans saw American mums and dads in peaceful protest being fired on they did their duty and built a wall to protect and serve.

Let's all protect and serve.

And listen.

In the same way seasoned feminists don't need male saviours, Black folk don't need white ones. They have their own leaders: follow them. And if they say they need something, give it to them. Don't take up the cause for any 'othered' group – join them – they're just as invisible as we were.

Together, we can't be missed.

# 23

# INVINCIBLE

*Together we win*

July 2020

> JANE
>
> You know I went to put a tweet up to
> celebrate us getting the book deal.
> I couldn't find a single gif with a
> white midlife woman celebrating with
> a Black woman.

> CAROL
>
> Really?

> JANE
>
> So then I searched Black queen and
> white queen.

> CAROL
>
> What did you get?

> JANE
>
> Black and white gifs of Beyoncé.

                        CAROL
        Fair enough. Did you try an
        image search?

                        JANE
        Chess pieces!


It's not just Black and white women who need to come together, we're all in this together and there's a lot of change ahead – it's time to make some noise.


        I am woman, hear me roar
        In numbers too big to ignore


Helen Reddy left us on 29 September 2020 and the woman who gave us the ultimate feminist anthem will never be forgotten. But her songwriting partner Ray Burton was forgotten the moment 'I Am Woman' hit the charts. It's totally understandable that Helen kept quiet about his contribution at the time; she certainly couldn't be seen singing 'I can do anything' to a man's tune.

It's no surprise we struggled with feminism in the early days when the 'feminists don't need men' narrative was so strong. For a large percentage of women that's a notion that goes against every ounce of our biology. Many of us have always enjoyed the love, friendship and support of good men.

We need the support of good men. And even though we know we haven't come as far as we'd have liked by now, we are getting closer to equal. It's time to really work together.


        And I know too much to go back an' pretend
        'Cause I've heard it all before
        And I've been down there on the floor
        No one's ever gonna keep me down again

It's great that men are standing up for us in the workplace, holding diversity initiatives, opening seats on panels and in the boardroom, but they will never be true allies until they actually start pulling their weight.

Women across the globe still do 75% of the unpaid care work, so even the most ardent male feminists really do have to do more and get real. Yes, we know they all do a hell of a lot more around the house than their fathers did but nowhere near as much as they think they do. In the early days of lockdown, a survey said that 49% of men took on 100% of the home-schooling. Only 3% of women agreed (probably while laughing their heads off!)

> Oh yes, I am wise
> But it's wisdom born of pain
> Yes, I've paid the price
> But look how much I gained

Men also need to take our lead in the ageism debate. Particularly privileged white midlife men. They hate being called that; they take it as an insult. We're privileged midlife women, one white, one Black, and take no offence to that honest description, but white men appear to be embarrassed by their privilege or else they genuinely believe they would be exactly where they are in life if they had been born a different gender or class or with another skin colour. Most of them have never faced an -ism in their life.

In advertising, only 6.3% of workers are over 50 (nobody dares give a gender breakdown so again, it's probably zero). White admen over 50 moan about their lot – a lot! They seem to have a sense of entitlement that they should continue in the roles they have always had and work in the way they've always worked. A way of working where they never seemed to notice when the white women they worked alongside disappeared, or that they'd never worked with a Black woman in an equal role. But now men face ageism, we women are supposed to treat their discrimination with the same importance as ours. Which is rich coming from men who have enjoyed long, uninterrupted careers and should, by now, have sizeable retirement pots.

Our response (with our tongue planted heavily in our cheek) is: 'Let's be a little old-fashioned about this, open the door, ladies first.'

We have a much better argument to build a new second half of our lives. Many of us believed our early careers were a sprint, now they've turned into a marathon, and this is where our biology comes into its own. This is the time when we are the natural leaders.

And we'll lead everyone to the place we've always been heading. One that's equal.

> If I have to, I can do anything
> I am strong
> I am invincible
> I am woman.

We are so much more powerful than we think.

Money makes the world go around. Right? Wouldn't it be nice to control the world's money?

We practically do!

Women over 45 buy 50% of everything and spend 2.5 times more than the average person. There is power in these numbers. If we organise, we can get the world to value us. Ever so nicely, ever so sweetly. In total silence. Because the reason we buy 50% of everything isn't that we're all mega-rich: it's because we pretty much buy everything for everyone.

With that power, we could easily buy a new world for everyone. But first, we HAVE to take the oxygen mask. It won't take much to get us sorted financially. We just need older women in the full-paid workforce at all levels. And all we have to do is ask.

Digital natives claim that social media has changed the way brands handle customer complaints. It hasn't; it's just got more public.

In Australia, in the early 1990s, a male and female creative team came up with a fantastic tampon ad. It was simply a super on the screen that said: 'What tampon does your lady use?' And showed various men umming and ahhing, until one really cute guy smiled and said, 'Meds, I pick them up when I do the shopping.'

Now, as you can imagine, that was quite shocking at the time. A small branch of the Queensland Women's Institute got their knickers in a knot that men were discussing women's private things. It took them three letters to get a million-dollar-plus campaign pulled. And the tampon brand got millions of dollars in free publicity from the media reports that encouraged a legion of young women to buy their product in defiance.

Women who grew into us.

As recently as 2019, two British ads were pulled after six letters pointing out they showed outdated gender roles. There's something we were taught in our early years and it's still true – the customer is always right. Brands will fall over backwards to avoid bad publicity, keep customers and make money. And these days you don't have to go to all the effort of writing a letter and going to the post office to buy a stamp. You could start right now. And no one even needs to know.

What if, before you made any major purchase – from a mascara to a Maserati – you visited the contact form on the seller's website or @ them on your Twitter feed to ask them what the company's record is of hiring older women at all levels in their workforce.

A hundred questions from older women will get their attention.

A thousand will have them running to recruitment agencies. And a few million will have them messaging you back asking you if you want a job.

Once we're secure and employed we can use our immense power to create or invest in all the businesses and products we need for a better world.

It may seem flippant to suggest that sending a few questions to people trying to flog you stuff can change the world. But consider this: consumer spending is the most important factor in a country's economy.

At a time where we face potential economic disaster, the biggest spending demographic is more important than ever. When the economy is being rebuilt, we have a unique opportunity to change what we buy. We already have: who would have predicted UGG boots and Crocs would have seen the biggest surge in internet traffic during the first weeks of lockdown? Or that sales of tops would skyrocket? Seems a hell of a lot of us were zooming in our knickers.

Even when we don't have much, we have the luxury of spending well. We don't need to buy a throwaway culture we weren't born into. We can lead the charge in sustainability by refusing the ultimately unsatisfying buzz of instant gratification and make our purchases last. We've all got pieces in our wardrobes that prove that quality is a great investment, most of it is swiped by our on-point daughters.

Most of us have cupboards filled with stuff; we don't have to add anything unless it adds to our joy or the planet. When the going is tough, we can choose to buy from our community because our spending will help people. And when people are hurting the last thing any of us want to see is extravagance. For years, marketers have been talking about brand purpose. They now have to do more than talk – they have to show what their customers mean to them.

Whatever our life situation or political beliefs, 2020 has

taught us the value of human life. They say beside every poison there lies a cure. In a world struggling to find truth, who thought we could ever be in a position to demand it? When we control almost half the consumer spending. YES. WE. CAN.

# 24

# INVALUABLE

## *A world where we are seen and heard*

April 2021

> JANE
> Uninvisibility just landed our first
> paying ad client! And it's a biggie!

> CAROL
> I have news too - I just sold my first
> international pilot!

> JANE
> Oh my God, we're overnight successes.

> CAROL
> Only took 10 years!

Most of us are lucky to have midlife women in our lives:
ask anyone about their mum, their aunt, their granny, their

mentor or their friend and their face will light up. No, we're not all perfect, and we will never agree on everything, but when we embrace our differences to fight the forces of invisibility, the world will discover a resource it's never seen before. One that is loved, revered and ready to clean up this whole sorry mess.

This is time for action not words. And we are women of our word.

The Uninvisibility Project started out as a social media platform to change the narrative for midlife women, and we have put everything we have written in this book into practice.

In September 2020 Mark Read, the CEO of WPP, one of the world's largest advertising groups, was quoted (somewhat out of context) as saying:

*'We have a very broad range of skills and if you look at our people – the average age of someone who works at WPP is less than 30 – they don't hark back to the 1980s, luckily.'*

The industry, or parts of Twitter and the trade press at least, was up in arms. Jane put out a very public call to say the Uninvisibility project wanted words. To his credit, Mark picked up the phone. He was expecting a fight. He got a whole heap of tend and befriend.

That call was followed by a long letter that put forward an idea that would solve two of his immediate problems: we could rapidly increase the percentage of midlife workers in his organisation while filling a skills gap the whole industry is grappling with. And it would help him out-perform his competitors, including some of the more vocal ones.

One of Mark's biggest critics during this saga was his predecessor turned competitor. There was definitely a lot of pot calling kettle going on, as illustrated by this July

2020 Ad News interview where the ex-CEO of WPP, Sir Martin Sorrell, described his new holding company's workforce:

*'The average age is about 33. On the media side, about 600 at business unit MightyHive, the average age is about 25. The reason that they're so young is that programmatic people are difficult to find and we tend to train them ourselves. We hire them from good schools and then we train them and put them into data analytics or programmatic.'*

We simply reminded Mark that the best school is the school of life. Why not train those graduates too? We teamed up with Brixton Finishing School, who run courses to find diverse young people from underprivileged backgrounds for these roles and within weeks Visible Start was born and funded by WPP. Now midlife women have the opportunity to train in digital media online, in their own time, and to enter a pipeline where there are real jobs and further training waiting with open arms.

Can you do something similar in your industry? In your community? Let's all work together to get us all working. But also, let's look after the people who fall through the cracks when the world is shaking.

We'd like to end this book with a story of hope. Like most of the pioneering women we have featured, they have a story and experience that has huge significance for the world we live in today. When we adapted to lockdown we knew there were many people doing it harder than us. Now we face such uncertainty, take heart in the story of two women who have been there, done that and survived.

## Maha and Muna Salfiti

On 28 September 2000, Muna Salfiti held hands with her three small children and prayed. She asked God to give her the courage to protect them. For the next five years, it was almost impossible to leave her house. There wasn't an invisible enemy lurking outside her door. There were snipers, bombs, rocks and deadly crossfire.

It's almost impossible to explain the 2000– 2005 Palestinian Intifada: the Arabic word translates as tremor, shivering, shuddering. The truth of what it was, how it happened and why it lasted so long is lost in a muddled mess from 80 years of propaganda built on thousands of years of myths.

As a young mother, how do you explain to your children to keep away from windows and not to go outside – not even the back door? And as Christians, how do you guide your children to follow in the footsteps of Jesus without setting foot on the very streets they were born to walk?

'I remember, the first time the Israeli soldiers invaded Ramallah, people were so scared and screaming in the streets and this was something that was really new for me to deal with and it's something that I can't explain because it involves lots of blood, lots of anger, lots of different things that I had to make my children understand at a young age, so that was really hard. But then it's something that we believe in, something that we have lived and something that we needed to fight for. Not everybody can hold a weapon. My weapon was education for my children.'

Muna's instinct was to learn everything she could about the situation, which she reported to her older sister, Maha, with such regularity that Maha described Muna as her own personal CNN. Six months in, they really started to worry. It is estimated that between 28 September 2000 and 7 March 2001, 41 Palestinian schools were closed or unable to operate and approximately 20,000 Palestinian students were missing out on their education.

So the two sisters joined with their friend, a maths teacher (the only subject they couldn't handle between them), and set up a home school for their close family's children. On the first day, 8 children crawled on their hands and knees to get there. The second day, 18 showed up. On the third, they had 50 children risking their lives in the hope of creating a better one.

In the midst of all this chaos and danger, Maha and Muna created some normality.

'My whole house was divided into rooms and classes. We divided the children into age groups and we had classes for the whole time. We even taught languages like French as well as the main subjects; social studies, science, maths, Arabic, English, everything, you name it, it was there and the children just loved it and wanted to join this school more than their regular schools. Even though we had discipline, we had order, we had schedules that we had to follow with recess, lunch and breaks. And it worked really well. It

still has an impact on the children, because they
felt that they really had to stand against whatever was forced upon us and they prevailed. They
got their education, they got everything.'

They even had a bullet flying through the
middle of class.

In the hardest of times, Maha and Muna drew
on the strength of her fellow Palestinians who
believe they will one day rise like phoenixes from
the ashes. They taught their children to deal
with life issues, to be strong and to stand up for
themselves.

Both women remember the intifada as being
very hard for them, and they did what they had
to do. But looking back – it was fun and inspirational, something that was really good for the
children and has become a joy to remember.

We wish the same for all of you.

This too shall pass. And we really can make things better.

# INFORMATION

## *Notes, references and workings*

### Introduction – *The women of our time*

Sonya Renne Taylor is a highly acclaimed poet, activist,
    author and leader. Her poem about the new normal
    swept the internet in April 2020. See https://www.
    sonyareneetaylor.com/
'Ageism is first detected in children as young as three.'
    See https://www.ncbi.nlm.nih.gov/pmc/articles/
    PMC7198741/
Steve Bannon quote – his views on the anti-patriarchy
    movement: See https://www.independent.co.uk/news/
    world/americas/us-politics/steve-bannon-trump-tea-
    party-anti-patriarchy-movement-times-bloomberg-
    breitbart-news-a8206426.html

### 1. Invisible – *The return of the invisible women*

In 2015 only 3% of the world's creative directors were
    women: https://www.3percentmovement.com/
    movement

'The average age in an ad agency is 33.9'. See https://
www.moreaboutadvertising.com/2019/04/ipa-census-
creative-agencies-contract-while-media-expands/
https://ipa.co.uk/news/agency-census-2019

Joan Ellis describes her own experiences in top London
advertising agencies, with a funny, fast-paced tale
set against a backdrop of Thatcher's Britain where
money trumped morals and lust was a must. See
https://www.amazon.co.uk/I-am-Ella-Buy-me/
dp/0993009107

And the fact is that women over 50 buy 47% of
everything. These figures have been extracted
from the Office of National statistics 2019
report on family spending. See https://www.
ons.gov.uk/peoplepopulationandcommunity/
personalandhouseholdfinances/expenditure/bulletins/
familyspendingintheuk/april2018tomarch2019. The
ONS statistics weren't divided by gender so we applied
the statistic that women over 50 make 95% of all
household purchasing decisions http://she-conomy.
com/facts-on-women

The Uninvisibility Project. See https://uninvisibility.com

### 3. Inquisition – Time to question everything

'The Bible was first written'. See https://www.bbc.co.uk/
religion/religions/christianity/texts/bible.shtml

'There are figurines of goddesses that date back to 25,000
BC'. See http://www.hiddenhistory.co.uk/2017/03/28/
venus-figurines

Did the Queen of Sheba exist? See https://www.ancient.eu/
Queen_of_Sheba/

Bilqis. See http://www.oxfordislamicstudies.com/article/
opr/t125/e351

Makeda. See https://www.newscientist.com/article/
  dn21976-genes-reveal-grain-of-truth-to-queen-of-sheba-
  story/
Stories of 6,000 youths born on the same day.
  See http://www.jewishencyclopedia.com/
  articles/13515-sheba-queen-of
Islamic legend of Bilqis. See http://www.bbc.co.uk/history/
  ancient/cultures/sheba_01.shtml
Ethiopian legend and the Ark of the Covenant.
  See https://www.smithsonianmag.com/travel/
  keepers-of-the-lost-ark-179998820/
'DNA of an African woman who lived 200,000
  years ago'. See https://www.sciencedaily.com/
  releases/2010/08/100817122405.htm

## 4. Interconnected – The past is the way to the future

Article in *New Scientist*, 18 April 2018 – 'The Origins of
  Sexism: How Men Came to Rule 12,000 Years Ago' by
  Anil Ananthaswamy and Kate Douglas
Quote from *The Troublesome Helpmate: A History of
  Misogyny in Literature* by Katharine M. Rogers,
  originally in *Ain't I a Woman: Black Women and
  Feminism* by bell hooks
'If women want a feminist revolution . . .'. From *Ain't I a
  Woman: Black Women and Feminism* by bell hooks
Background reading for this chapter: *Common Differences:
  Conflicts in Black and White Feminist Perspectives* by Gloria
  I. Joseph and Jill Lewis; *Ain't I a Woman: Black Women
  and Feminism* by bell hooks, titled after Sojourner Truth's
  'Ain't I a Woman?' speech

### 5. Inheritance – We are all the women who have come before us

Christopher Vogler's memo. See https://livingspirit.typepad.
   com/files/chris-vogler-memo-1.pdf
*The Hero with a Thousand Faces* by Joseph Campbell
'We bled without dying and miraculously created humans'
   from *The Women's History of the World* by Rosalind Miles
All information on goddesses has been taken from Patricia
   Monaghan's *Goddesses and Heroines*, published in 1981 by
   E.P. Dutton Publishing Co.
The roots for the Dance of the Seven Veils are deemed
   by some to be in the ancient Sumerian or Babylonian
   legends of the goddess Inanna or Ishtar. She has to
   descend to the netherworld passing through seven
   gates in search of Tammuz. At each of them, she is
   required to shed one symbol of her status. She finally
   reaches the 'land of no return' as her pure self. This
   journey is possibly a metaphor for enlightenment
   that comes from shedding the veils of illusion. The
   journey itself is one that is into the self/self-realisation.
   The seven veils are suggested to be Dreams,
   Reason, Passion, Bliss, Courage, Compassion and
   Knowledge. See https://beyonder.travel/information/
   dance-of-the-seven-veils-striptease-and-travel/
The witchcraft hunts of northern Europe and North
   America raged from 1450 until 1750. See http://www.
   faculty.umb.edu/gary_zabel/Courses/Phil%20281b/
   Philosophy%20of%20Magic/Arcana/Witchcraft%20
   and%20Grimoires/case_witchhunts.html
Janet Horne – last woman executed for witchcraft.
   See https://www.nls.uk/learning-zone/
   literature-and-language/themes-in-focus/witches/
   source-6

The Witchcraft Act was finally repealed in 1951. See
https://www.parliament.uk/about/living-heritage/
transformingsociety/private-lives/religion/overview/
witchcraft/

Research into epigenetics shows that trauma attaches or
removes chemical tags to our DNA. See https://www.
bbc.com/future/article/20190326-what-is-epigenetics

'Soul Wounds'. See https://icmglt.org/wp-content/
uploads/2019/09/21-Healing-the-American-Indian-Soul-
Wound-.pdf

British girls were only given the right to an education in
1880. See https://www.oxford-royale.com/articles/
history-womens-education-uk/#aId=26d22ced-4760-
4127-bec1-296bd8205661

Women were writing in the eighth century. See https://www.
theguardian.com/books/2019/nov/07/womens-writing-
began-much-earlier-than-supposed-finds-academic

Joanne (JK) Rowling's nom de plume. See https://www.
capitalfm.com/news/jk-rowling-full-name/

University of Copenhagen used artificial
intelligence. See https://www.futurity.org/
adjectives-gender-descriptions-books-2143682-2/

## 6. Incomparable – There have never been women like us before

Joseph Banks, the botanist on Captain Cook's early
voyages, noted: https://www.sl.nsw.gov.au/
joseph-banks-endeavour-journal

The 2004 film 'What the bleep do we know!?' https://
whatthebleep.com/

The Great Southern land was discovered
in 1606: https://www.nla.gov.au/faq/
who-was-the-first-european-to-land-on-australia

In 1950, the world average life expectancy was 48
    years old. See https://www.who.int/whr/1998/
    media_centre/50facts/en/

For a white English woman it was 72. See https://
    www.ons.gov.uk/peoplepopulationandcommunity/
    birthsdeathsandmarriages/lifeexpectancies/articles/
    howhaslifeexpectancychangedovertime/2015-09-09

Average life expectancy for British women. See https://www.
    theguardian.com/society/2020/mar/03/life-expectancy-
    in-england-rebounds-after-years-of-stagnation

In the United States, childbirth is the sixth biggest killer
    of women aged between 20 and 34. See https://slate.
    com/technology/2013/09/death-in-childbirth-doctors-
    increased-maternal-mortality-in-the-20th-century-are-
    midwives-better.html

Britain passed the Sex Disqualification (Removal) Act. See
    https://www.legislation.gov.uk/ukpga/Geo5/9-10/71/
    section/1

In 1970, 35% of UK women were still elbow-deep in the
    laundry tub. See https://www.statista.com/statistics/
    289017/washing-machine-ownership-in-the-uk/

Equal pay for equal work. See https://tuc150.tuc.org.uk/
    stories/dagenham-womens-strike/

Sex Discrimination Act receives royal assent 12
    November 1975. See https://www.legislation.gov.uk/
    ukpga/1975/65/enacted

Queen's 'Bohemian Rhapsody' hits Number 1 on 23
    November 1975. See https://www.popexpresso.
    com/2019/11/23/in-1975-queens-bohemian-rhapsody-
    charts-at-no-1-for-the-first-time/

'If there isn't a seat at the table, bring a folding chair.'
    Shirley Chisholm 1968. See https://www.npr.
    org/2018/11/06/664617076/a-look-back-on-shirley-
    chisholm-s-historic-1968-house-victory

Women weren't officially included in medical research until
    1993. See https://www.ncbi.nlm.nih.gov/pmc/articles/
    PMC4800017/

When scientists at UCLA discovered the fight or flight reflex.
    See https://www.nytimes.com/2000/05/19/us/scientists-
    find-a-particularly-female-response-to-stress.html

TikTok teens trash Trump rally in Tulsa. See https://www.
    nytimes.com/2020/06/21/style/tiktok-trump-rally-tulsa.
    html

TikTok grandma. See https://www.forbes.com/sites/
    larrymagid/2020/06/21/how-a-51-year-old-
    grandmother-and-thousands-of-teens-used-tiktok-to-
    derail-a-trump-rally--maybe-save-lives/

### 7. Interlopers – White women get to work

Lyn Middlehurst was creative director of KHBB
    (part of Saatchi & Saatchi) 1982– 8. For the last
    29 years she has travelled the world producing the
    Gallivanter's Guide. See https://www.linkedin.com/in/
    lyn-middlehurst-67a8529/

Barbara Nokes. See https://www.campaignlive.co.uk/
    article/unsung-women-advertising/1494742

'You can only sleep your way to the middle.' Keynote at
    COW (Creative Opportunities for Women) Sydney,
    Australia 1996

Sexual harassment amendment to the Sex Discrimination
    Act 1986. See https://www.legislation.gov.uk/
    ukpga/1986/59/enacted

In 1995 creative women dominated the Australian
    advertising award scene. See https://www.bandt.com.au/
    women-in-medias-jane-evans-i-was-one-of-the-first-girls-
    in-the-creative-department-my-whole-career-has-been-a-
    fight/

Jane Caro AM. See https://en.wikipedia.org/wiki/
    Jane_Caro
29% of US Creative Directors are women. See https://
    www.3percentmovement.com/mission
17% of UK Creative Directors are women. See https://www.
    creativeequals.org/

## 8. Inspiration – Black women fight to work

Toni Morrison quote from 'Toni Morrison's flight to
    freedom', *The Scarlet*, 6 December 2019. See https://
    thescarlet.org/16726/lartSToni-morrisons-flight-to-
    freedom-asserting-a-legendary-legacy/
Background reading for this chapter:
*Heart of the Race: Black Women's Lives in Britain* by Beverley
    Bryan, Stella Dadzie and Suzanne Scafe; *The Life of Una
    Marson* by Delia Jarret Macauley'; and 'All discovering
    literature: 20th-Century People' – British Library
    article

## 9. Intuition – The world needs our wisdom and experience

Satoshi Watanabe quote from Kidiyo Kpalma, Joseph
    Ronsin, *An Overview of Advances of Pattern Recognition
    Systems in Computer Vision*. Prof. Goro Obinata and
    Dr Ashish Dutta. Vision Systems, Advanced Robotic
    Systems, p.26, 2007
On wisdom and seeing patterns: 'The branching of
    dendrites [in the brain] increases [with age], and
    connections between distant brain areas strengthen.
    These changes enable the ageing brain to become
    better at detecting relationships between diverse
    sources of information, capturing the big picture,

and understanding the global implications of
specific issues. Perhaps this is the foundation of
wisdom. It is as if, with age, your brain becomes
better at seeing the entire forest . . .' See https://
www.health.harvard.edu/mind-and-mood/
how-memory-and-thinking-ability-change-with-age

*Love Thy Neighbour.* TV programme, 1972–6. See https://
www.imdb.com/title/tt0068096/

*Tatler* magazine, originally targeting upper echelons of
society. See https://www.tatler.com/

## 10. Indivisible – When wise women come together, we all come together

The Equal Rights Amendment and Mrs Phyllis Schafly.
See https://www.latimes.com/entertainment-artSTv/
story/2020-07-30/steinem-and-smeal-why-mrs-america-
is-bad-for-american-women

Divorce statistics UK: https://www.relate.org.uk/sites/
default/files/separation-divorce-factsheet-jan2014.pdf

In Australia, women over 55 are the fastest-growing group
of homeless. See https://www.smh.com.au/national/
having-to-ask-for-somewhere-to-live-it-s-difficult-indeed-
single-female-homeless-australia-s-shameful-crisis-
20200127-p53uyg.html

Pensions not discussed in divorce cases. See CII Investment
in Women's Futures Research, 2019.

*Ain't I a Woman? Black Women and Feminism,* bell hooks,
1981

*The Beauty Myth* by Naomi Wolf, originally published 1990

'Women who run with the wolves' reference from Clarissa
Pinkola Estés' iconic book of the same name

References: *Lean In* by Sheryl Sandberg; *Fear of Flying* by
Erica Jong; *Fire with Fire* by Naomi Wolf

The suffragettes first mass petition in 1866. See
   https://www.parliament.uk/about/living-heritage/
   transformingsociety/electionsvoting/womenvote/
   parliamentary-collections/1866-suffrage-petition/
   presenting-the-petition/

The 19 types of feminism referenced here are: Mainstream
   feminism, Anarchist, Black and womanist,
   Cultural, Difference, Ecofeminism, French, Liberal,
   Libertarian, Multiracial, Post-structural, Postcolonial,
   Postmodern, Radical, Separatist and lesbian,
   Socialist and Marxist, Standpoint, Third-world,
   Transfeminism. See: https://en.wikipedia.org/wiki/
   Feminist_movements_and_ideologies

Maggie Lawrence, 'Reproductive Rights and State
   Institutions: The Forced Sterilization of Minority Women
   in the United States', Senior Theses, Trinity College,
   Hartford, CT, 2014. Trinity College Digital Repository.
   See http://digitalrepository.trincoll.edu/theses/390

Women of colour in FTSE 100 and 250: https://www.
   ft.com/content/409ae838-1040-11e9-b2f2-f4c566a4fc5f

The term 'Womanist' comes from Alice Walker's 1979 short
   story 'Coming Apart' and published in *You Can't Keep A
   Good Woman Down*, Houghton Mifflin Harcourt, 1981

Mystical meaning of the word crone. See https://www.
   cronescounsel.org/the-ancient-crone/

## 11. Incommunicado – Time for a cuppa

Almost 300 million midlife women are currently
   on Facebook. See https://www.statista.com/
   statistics/376128/facebook-global-user-age-distribution/

Russian troll farms. See https://www.
   rollingstone.com/politics/politics-features/
   russia-troll-2020-election-interference-twitter-916482/

#MeToo, the movement to eliminate sexual violence. See
   https://metoomvmt.org/


## 12. Intermediate – It's not just young and old – there's a whole new middle

Healthy boomers could live to 120. See https://time.
   com/4835763/how-long-can-humans-live/
The sum total of human knowledge. See https://www.
   industrytap.com/knowledge-doubling-every-12-months-
   soon-to-be-every-12-hours/3950
Mark Zuckerberg, 'Are Young People Smarter?'
   *Forbes*, 2 February 2015. See https://www.
   forbes.com/sites/stevenkotler/2015/02/14/
   is-silicon-valley-ageist-or-just-smart/
Tim Berners-Lee, July 2018, *Vanity Fair*. See https://www.
   vanityfair.com/news/2018/07/the-man-who-created-the-
   world-wide-web-has-some-regrets
From 'I Invented the Web, Here's How We Can Fix
   It,' by Tim Berners-Lee. See https://www.nytimes.
   com/2019/11/24/opinion/world-wide-web.html
'Advertising'. From *Girl's Companion's Career Guide*, first
   published 1947 by Blackie & Son Ltd
Americans over fifty felt ten years younger. See
   https://www.pewsocialtrends.org/2009/06/29/
   growing-old-in-america-expectations-vs-reality/


## 13. Instantaneous – The world has changed to meet us

Rise in domestic violence during lockdown. See https://
   www.theguardian.com/society/2020/nov/05/
   fears-grow-domestic-abuse-england-enters-second-
   lockdown

Working from home statistics. See https://www.finder.com/
uk/working-from-home-statistics

79% of businesses carried on through lockdown. See
https://www.ons.gov.uk/businessindustryandtrade/
business/businessservices/bulletins/
coronavirusandtheeconomicimpactsontheuk/21may2020

Employees who want to continue working from home. See
https://www.independent.co.uk/news/uk/home-news/
coronavirus-office-return-employees-workers-social-
distancing-pandemic-a9693796.html

Working remotely projections. See https://www.bbc.co.uk/
news/business-54482245

*Fast Company*: We are approaching the fastest, deepest,
most consequential technological disruption in
history. See www.fastcompany.com/90559711/
we-are-approaching-the-fastest-deepest-most-
consequential-technological-disruption-in-history

*Rethinking Humanity* by James Arbib and Tony Seba. See
https://www.rethinkx.com/humanity

'Global Recessions' by M. Ayhan Kose, Naotaka Sugawara
and Marco E. Terrones. See http://documents1.
worldbank.org/curated/en/185391583249079464/pdf/
Global-Recessions.pdf

The future of jobs and skills. See https://
reports.weforum.org/future-of-jobs-2016/
chapter-1-the-future-of-jobs-and-skills/

'Top ten soft skills needed in today's workplace' by
Marcel M Robles. See https://www.researchgate.net/
publication/258126575_Executive_Perceptions_of_the_
Top_10_Soft_Skills_Needed_in_Today's_Workplace

$700 billion invested in age tech each year: See https://www.
forbes.com/siteSTinawoods/2019/02/01/age-tech-the-
next-frontier-market-for-technology-disruption/

## 14. Intermission – Menopause: it's just a rewire and reboot

Pyjamas made of thermal materials. See https://
www.womansworld.com/gallery/menopause/
best-menopause-pajamas-for-women-over-50-168240
Bras that monitor emotions. See https://www.bbc.co.uk/
news/technology-25197917

## 15. Insouciance – The other side of the change

Older women's brains look similar to younger mens. See
https://qz.com/1543082/older-womens-brains-look-
similar-to-younger-mens/
Women make up 39% of global employment but account
for 54% of overall job losses. See https://www.
mckinsey.com/featured-insights/future-of-work/covid-
19-and-gender-equality-countering-the-regressive-
effects
60% of all employees in the UK now work from home. See
https://www.finder.com/uk/working-from-home-
statistics
70% of childrearing and household chores. See https://www.
sciencedaily.com/releases/2019/01/190122092857
.htm
When orcas and pilot whales go through menopause, they
become the leaders of their pods. See https://www.
scientificamerican.com/article/a-new-theory-for-why-
killer-whales-go-through-menopause/
One in five women is still concerned about going back
to work after maternity leave. See https://www.
peoplemanagement.co.uk/news/articles/fewer-than-
one-in-five-women-confident-return-maternity-
leave

In Australia, 50% of all women over 70 and 34% of single women over 50 are already below the breadline. See https://www.sbs.com.au/topics/voices/culture/article/2017/11/24/aged-over-60-and-female-heres-why-you-might-be-risk-poverty

## 16. Incurable – We're not getting any younger

One in three American women are considering getting work done, 26% of whom said it was down to 'Wanting to appear youthful at work' or 'Looking for or starting a new job'. See https://www.marketwatch.com/story/one-in-four-people-is-considering-plastic-surgery-to-look-younger-at-work-2018-09-26

A third of the long-term unemployed are over 50. See https://www.peoplemanagement.co.uk/news/articles/over-50s-more-likely-to-face-long-term-unemployment

Diane Keaton quote. See https://blog.aarp.org/be-your-best/diane-keaton-has-7-ways-to-age-with-attitude

Lauren Bacall quote. See https://www.forbes.com/quotes/5892/

Paulina Porizkova quote. See http://www.dailymagazine.news/paulina-porizkova-on-filtered-reality-aging-gracefully-and-the-one-cosmetic-treatment-she-s-loving-right-now-nid-661225.html

Anita Roddick quote. See https://www.telegraph.co.uk/news/uknews/1370925/Wrinkle-cream-is-pap-says-Roddick.html

La Mer copy. See https://www.lamer.co.nz/creme-de-lamer

£65,000 richer at 70 calculation based on: Boots Simple Kind to Skin Rich Moisturiser Replenishing 125ml £4.29 = £3.43 per 100ml vs L'Oréal Paris Revitalift Laser Renew Anti-Ageing Day Cream 15ml £6.99 = £46.60 per 100ml. 100ml of moisturiser should last 90

days, even if it is fairly generous use. This will result in
purchase 4 times a year. Boots Simple: spend £13.72
per year. Over 40 years = £548.80 (note this does not
take account of inflation or price increases over time).
L'Oréal Paris: spend £186.40 per year. Over 40 years,
spend is £7,456. Difference between the two: in one year:
£172.68; over 40 years: £6,907.20. How does that affect
a pension? Let's say you have a pension with a rate of 9%,
then after 40 years you have £65,538.48.

Dame Anita Roddick obituary. See https://www.
    independent.co.uk/news/obituaries/dame-anita-roddick-
    402053.html
All Roddick quotes from Anita Roddick, *Business as Unusual*
    (2000)
Michelle Thew quote. See https://www.independent.co.uk/
    news/people/profiles/how-anita-changed-the-world-
    402108.html

## 17. Infiltrate – Let's get to work

Centre for Better Ageing Report. See https://www.
    ageing-better.org.uk/sites/default/files/2020-08/Tackling-
    worklessness-among-over-50s-after-covid-report.pdf
Unemployment in the United Kingdom averaged
    6.87% from 1971 until 2020, reaching an all-
    time high of 11.90% in April of 1984. Source:
    https://tradingeconomics.com/united-kingdom/
    unemployment-rate
A third of unemployed midlife women face long-
    term unemployment. See https://www.
    peoplemanagement.co.uk/news/articles/
    over-50s-more-likely-to-face-long-term-unemployment
Women only have a third of men's retirement savings and 1.2
    million of us in Britain have no private pension savings at

all. See https://www.independent.co.uk/news/business/
news/pension-savings-gap-childcare-gender-pay-gap-
women-a9000066.html

Sylvia Rivera quote. See https://herdacity.org/sylvia-rivera/

Amplification on Barack Obama's team. See
https://www.vox.com/2016/9/14/12914370/
white-house-obama-women-gender-bias-amplification

Shine theory. See https://www.shinetheory.com/

It will take 202 years to close the global gender pay gap.
See https://www.theguardian.com/world/2018/dec/18/
global-gender-pay-gap-will-take-202-years-to-close-says-
world-economic-forum

Men earning over £150,000 outnumbered women 5:1 and
ten times more make over a million. See https://www.
thetimes.co.uk/article/men-earning-over-150-000-
outnumber-women-5-1-5sqtjnx6f

The 2,153 billionaires across the world, only 252 are women.
See https://www.forbes.com/sites/forbespr/2019/03/05/
press-release-forbes-33rd-annual-worlds-billionaires-
issue-reveals-number-of-billionaires-and-their-combined-
wealth-have-decreased-for-for-first-time-since-2016/

The three Black female billionaires. See https://
face2faceafrica.com/article/did-you-know-there-are-only-
three-black-female-billionaires-in-the-world

There are more people over 65 than children under 5. See
https://www.nationalgeographic.com/culture/2019/07/
global-population/

## 18. Invest – It's time to put our money where our future is

In 2019, out of $104 billion in venture capital funding. See
https://techcrunch.com/2019/07/06/startups-weekly-
2019-vc-spending-may-eclipse-2018-record/

2.7% funding for female founders. See https://fortune.
com/2020/03/02/female-founders-funding-2019/

1% funding for women of colour. See https://www.
createcultivate.com/blog/black-female-investors

Dorothy L. Sayers quote. See https://www.goodreads.com/
quotes/191320-time-and-trouble-will-tame-an-advanced-
young-woman-but

A startup founded by someone over 50 is 2.2 times more
likely to succeed than one founded by a 30-year-old. See
https://www.inc.com/jeff-haden/a-study-of-27-million-
startups-found-ideal-age-to-start-a-business-and-its-much-
older-than-you-think.html

Women over 55 make the best bosses. See https://www.
telegraph.co.uk/goodlife/11618322/Its-official-women-
over-55-make-the-best-bosses.html

Age tech worth $2 trillion. See https://www.longevity.
technology/agetech-start-ups-uk-market-players/

## 20. Innovate – It's a whole new world that needs new things

Teens in AI. See https://www.teensinai.com/

*Let It Go*, Dame Stephanie Shirley, Penguin 2019

81% of business coaches fail. See https://milliondollarcoach.
com/blog/81-coaches-fail/

The Writer's Guild of America has around 20,000
members but only 2,188 screenwriters got paying
work in 2019. See https://deadline.com/2020/07/
wga-west-members-earned-a-record-1-68-billion-last-
year-under-guild-contracts-over-scale-payments-for-
agentless-writer-producers-not-reflected-in-data-
1202991983/

### 21. Initiate – Start something. Anything

How to help out food banks. See https://onecantrust.org.uk/

The social imagination. See https://www.geoffmulgan.com/
post/social-imagination

Haile Selassi's speech to the UN, 1963. See https://
face2faceafrica.com/article/read-emperor-haile-selassies-
iconic-1963-speech-that-inspired-bob-marleys-hit-song-war

*Salon* magazine 2002. See https://www.salon.
com/2002/10/12/sinead_3/

Source for *Washington Post* thought piece. See https://blog.
usejournal.com/snl-owes-sin%C3%A9ad-oconnor-an-
apology-a79174a45fdd

'Nothing Compares 2 U', written by Prince

### 22. Intervene – Standing up for what we believe in

*Lord of the Flies*, William Golding, originally published 1954

Captain Peter Warner. See https://www.theguardian.com/
world/2020/may/13/the-real-lord-of-the-flies-mano-
totau-survivor-story-shipwreck-tonga-boys-ata-island-
peter-warner

### 23. Invincible – Together we win

Women across the globe still do 75% of the unpaid care
work. *Invisible Women* by Caroline Criado Perez, Chatto
& Windus, 2019

Men claim to do 100% of home-schooling. See https://www.
nytimes.com/2020/05/06/upshot/pandemic-chores-
homeschooling-gender.html

In advertising only 6.3% of workers are over 50. See https://
www.moreaboutadvertising.com/2019/04/ipa-census-
creative-agencies-contract-while-media-expands/

## 24. Invaluable – A world where we are seen and heard

Mark Read Head of WPP comments. See https://www.
  thetimes.co.uk/article/row-over-ageist-remarks-forces-
  apology-from-wpp-boss-mark-read-rx03z5p3g
Sir Martin Sorrell's comments. See
  https://www.adnews.com.au/news/
  s4-capital-plans-to-poach-key-people-from-competitors

# INDEBTEDNESS

*All the people who got us here*

### Jane's thank yous

To Ella Bee and Maya Hart, my ever-patient daughters, who have been on this roller-coaster ride all the way. I am so proud of the young women you have become despite all the setbacks we have faced. I wish it could have been easier. You are strong, creative and courageous. I can't wait to see your stories unfold.

To Terry Comer. Thank you for the sanctuary and peace of mind to write this book. And the jokes you still whisper in my ear.

Gemma Higgins, for just being the incredible soul and champion you are. And for the inspiration, the research, the editing and for lending me Daffy to keep me walking on the tightrope when everything was on fire.

Jacquie Duckworth, my partner in crime, Uninvisibility would be invisible without you.

Ruby. A blessing by name and a blessing by (and from) nature. Could never have gone this far without you and your dreams too.

Karen Lane, whether around the corner or on the other side of the world, you've always been there for me. Thank you.

Sam Tannous – the complete package – best friend, personal editor and glitter-auntie to the girls.

To the women on whose shoulders I stand. My mum for being pure love. My grandmother who I wish I'd spent more time with and my godmother Dr Phillida Frost, one of the UK's first female anaesthetists, who taught me from a very early age there was more to life than housework.

Djurunpinjinbah. For teaching me how to fly (and more importantly, land!).

Yehuda Goldfiner. For tuning in.

Gayle Rich. For teaching me how to tune in.

Mara Marich. For always setting the bar so high.

Andy Orrick. For making everything whole.

Janetta Lewin, Sue Higgs, Mady Morris and Sara Stoneham. This ball would have never got rolling without you.

Ellie Butler, for being there when I didn't even know what this was.

Michelle Little, Rubi Khan, Adah Paris, Beck Brideson, Kathryn Chapman, Jill Greenberg, Janet Grey, Tania Lacy, Kay Scorah, Stephanie Chapel, Anonymous and Heidi Chase, whose stories are the foundation for everything.

Cindy Gallop, for leading the charge and giving me the courage to shout from the rooftops.

Dame Cilla Snowball, Sue Unerman, Kathryn Jacob OBE, Helen Brain, Claire Davidson, Zoe Scaman, Lucy Bunce, Ally Owen and all the amazing businesswomen who blazed the trail for Uninvisibility.

Vikki Ross, for always having the perfect words.

Antoinette De Lisser, who believed in me when no one in the industry did.

Michelle Nicol, for making sure I never ran out of necessities. For the Facebook Group #Iamremarkable for really being there, same for NABS, Southwark Council, my MP Helen Hayes and all the wonderful people who donated to

Uninvisibility's Go Fund Me set up when three of us were in immediate peril. We're all safe now. Thank you.

To all my heroes: my dad. Martin Evans, Charlie, Max and Joe. Mr Weir. Christen Monge. Tom Horton. Captain Geraldo de Rosa, Brian Jones. Tom Upstone. Chuck Hahn. Rhett Sampson.

To Mike Allain, Hilary Mantle, Dana Minter, Mike Doyle, Carolyn Diamond, Jane Caro and Jack Vaughan, who all taught this art director how to write. To Peter Ansorge, who taught me how to tell a story, sat me next to the best writing partner on the planet, and to Lord Michael Grade, who loved the start of my tale and was fascinated to see how it would end. We hope good sirs, this is to your satisfaction.

To all the amazing humans I have met through the invisibility project both in real life and zoom.

To everyone who kept us and the hope alive.

And to everyone who ever shared their story with me, you are all part of this one and all of those to come.


### Carol's thank yous

To Ian Macdonald, for keeping me fed and watered through a long hot summer.

To Judith Bryan, Amanda Parker and Leone Ross, for the hours spent chatting about the joys and tribulations of being midlife women of African descent living in a world that doesn't always appreciate us. This is our time.

To Julie Clare, who kept me sane and fed me with laughter.

To my sister-in-law, Karen Russell, who is a Karen by name, but not by nature.

To Diane Abbott, for living an exemplary life and showing all us Caribbean women how to persevere.

To Juanne Fuller, who knows how to raise midlife women up to the heights.

To Pat Cumper, Carmen Harris, Eva Edo and Juliet Gilkes Romero, my midlife posse of writers, who give me the strength and the will to go on.

To Rayna Cambell who was always there with an encouraging word.

To Barbara Emile, who guides me through the TV industry with a torch that is more like a floodlight.

To Paulette Randall, who gave me my start as a writer.

To Linnet Farquarson, for always being willing to listen to me as I witter on and hold me up when I think I'm down and out.

To Vivienne Harvey, I owe you more than words can say.

To my brother, who keeps my feet on the ground – always!

And even though they've crossed the river to the other side, to my mother, Mavis Russell, Aunt Kathy, Auntie Vera, Auntie Lily, Auntie Caro and my grandmother, Doris Francis Richards, for all having a hand in making me the woman I am today.

And to all the women of African descent whose names I don't know who were here before me. Because of all of you, I can.